Laura Thompson read English at Oxford. Her first book, *The Dogs*, won the Somerset Maugham Award. While living in Newmarket she wrote two books about horse racing, followed by a biography of Nancy Mitford and a major study of Agatha Christie, reissued in 2018 in the US. Her book about Lord Lucan, *A Different Class of Murder*, was also reissued in 2018.

Take Six Girls, a group biography of the Mitford sisters, published in the US in 2016, was a *New York Times* bestseller. Her most recent book, *Rex v Edith Thompson*, about the Thompson-Bywaters murder case of the early 1920s, has been longlisted for a CWA Gold Dagger award.

By the Same Author

THE LAST LANDLADY

This edition first published in 2018

Unbound
6th Floor Mutual House, 70 Conduit Street, London W1S 2GF
www.unbound.com

Text design by PDQ

A CIP record for this book is available from the British Library

ISBN 978-1-78352-502-7 (trade hbk)
ISBN 978-1-78352-503-4 (ebook)
ISBN 978-1-78352-501-0 (limited edition)

Printed in Great Britain by CPI Group (UK)

THE LAST LANDLADY

Laura Thompson

An English Memoir

Unbound

'It was astonishing how significant, coherent and understandable it all became after a glass of wine on an empty stomach... One realized all sorts of things. The value of an illusion, for instance, and that the shadow can be more important than the substance.'

From *Quartet* by Jean Rhys

'There is nothing which has yet been contrived by man, by which so much happiness is produced as by a good tavern or inn.'

From Boswell's *Life of Johnson*

I

When I think of my grandmother, it is thus: seated on a high stool, her stool, in the negligent but alert position of a nightclub singer. Behind her, a cool brick wall, whose edges made little snags in the satin shirts that she wore loose over trousers. One of her hands rested on her thigh, not quite relaxed, holding a glass.

Her hair was white but not a grandmotherly white. She went regularly to the salon on the top floor at Harrods, a fairyland pink parlour in those days, its air dense and shimmering with little starbursts of Elnett. She would come home with tales of her hairdresser's love life (somewhat pitiable) and green and gold bags full of Estée Lauder cosmetics. From middle age onwards she disdained most products that were not by Estée Lauder, and there was never any arguing with her. The collars of her shirts were impregnated with Alliage scent, and the Re-Nutriv cold cream on her dressing table bore the marks of her fingers dragged across its surface, like little furrows in snow. She wore dark foundation and a deep red lipstick. Even now I feel that I am letting her down if I do not paint my lips.

So here she is: a casual empress on her stool, a woman in late middle age with a brightness, an intensity of being, that still flares in my head. Mysteriously moving, to feel memory shaping her as I write... which reminds me quite suddenly of a camera that she owned, a huge thing with a blue flashlight on top. After the blinding click the photo would ooze slowly out of the camera, a hot square with a white frame around indeterminate dark blobs. My grandmother would clamp it beneath her arm, waiting for it to develop against the warmth of her body. If it didn't flatter her, she would simply throw it away, ripped quickly in two, before anybody else could see it.

Because of her instant culls, many snapped moments are lost, which I suppose is a pity, but I rather like it that way. Photos are finite and unarguable. I prefer the images that are stored in the mind, the precious surprises that they spring (which of course you are springing upon yourself), their magical areas of occlusion and sharpness. Quite unexpectedly I can see, for instance, the slightly pigeon-toed angle of my grandmother's feet, looking older than the rest of her, placed upon the bar of her stool. I can see how she was framed, by the open wooden door to her left, and the counter on which she would lean her right forearm. I can see the texture of the counter, although I have no idea what it was made of (I might know now; these are childhood memories). It was shiny, orange-coppery in colour, hammered with tiny dents, wet where one least expected it to be. And it was covered with the evening's ecstatic confusion: beer mats, glasses, a sturdy blue-green ice bucket, a couple of siphons, the large square ashtray into which my grandmother stubbed her Player's untipped.

Her glass, which was her own thick tumbler, contained whisky and soda. She loved alcohol with a respectful, tender passion, and nursed the glass rather as she did her little dogs (she owned chihuahuas, years before they became fashionable), although she drank from it only occasionally. Just a deep sip, now and again, to maintain her *dégagée* buoyancy. She had learned to phrase her personality, as a singer phrases a lyric; she knew the power of withholding, and of brief conspiratorial bursts of charm. People bought her drinks all the time, seeking to please, and she usually accepted them. She would raise her glass in thanks ('Cheers, darling!'), put it to her mouth, and then throw the contents on the floor. A strip of carpet beside her stool was permanently damp with whisky. Although she did her drink-chucking surreptitiously, as she believed, everybody knew that she did it. It was part of her legend, like her stage whispers and her London childhood.

Around her shining silvered head – the beacon of the pub – the picture is vaguer. She was the person who conjured and orchestrated everything, so naturally the spotlight of memory follows her around. For example, I see again how, when the evenings were busy, she would slide unobtrusively from her stool in the public bar to the other side of the counter, and instantly take up the role of barmaid-in-chief. As she did so, the way in which drinks were served changed, became theatrical. She tugged at beer handles and shoved glasses under optics, hacked at lemons and ripped off bottle tops, all with an untidy, efficient grandeur that invested every drink with a particular potency.

People would sip reverentially, eyes briefly closed. 'Oh, that's lovely, Vi.' This may not have been illusory; the strength of her drinks was also legendary (her gin and French was akin to a knockout punch). Her horror of smallness, exactitude, led her to throw in extra measures of spirits, ice, whatever was going. Meanwhile the round would grow, it sometimes seemed exponentially, or possibly eternally, if the buyer was generous: people who had been served first would be finishing their drink while the round was still in play, so in theory this was a situation that could go on for ever. 'You'd better have another one, boy, while I'm in the mood.' 'Go on then, boy, if you say so.'

Oh yes, they're *good* drinkers, my grandmother would say the next day, in a tone of the utmost seriousness.

'Have you got one?' 'Yes, I've got one!' 'What about you, have you got one, girl?' 'Oh, I'm all right.' 'I know you're all right, but have you *got one?*'

The till behind the counter was a hefty chunk of Bakelite, grey and immovable, with a drawer that regularly jammed but could flatten your breasts when it deigned to spring open, and powerful keys that bore the symbols of numbers but did nothing so *recherché* as adding them up. Therefore alongside the lemons and cherries behind the bar were dank little notepads, on which the cost of a round might be calculated.

This was not really my grandmother's style. She had never gone to school, or so she said (in fact she spent several terms at a London convent, perhaps the only girl named Solomon ever to have done so), and she never got to grips with decimalisation. She could have done, but she could not be bothered. '55p' for a shot of gin meant ten bob, sort of; thus the niminy-piminy increases demanded with every Budget were absorbed into her large-scale nature. Thus, too, the giant rounds that formed the climax of so many evenings were totted up and rounded down to a sum that she thought acceptable. 'Call it a tenner, darling.' 'How do you make that out, Violet?' my father would say, in a droll tone that added to the general delight at seeing her legend in action. God knows how many Estée Lauder lipsticks she missed out on with these habitual underestimates. Often people would remonstrate with her, demanding that she take more money, forcing pound notes into her recalcitrant hands. These were the right sort of people, her sort, the kind who fought to pay more while she fought to take less. If the wrong sort came in to the pub, she could become surprisingly mean. In the early evenings she would lay out free food on the counter: the centrepiece was a huge wedge of Cheddar, stabbed in the heart with a cheese knife, surrounded by an overlapping necklace of Ritz crackers. Tacitly, it was understood that this was for regulars. Passing trade might take a sliver of cheese, a gherkin or two, not more. Every now and again some hapless person, who did not know the code of the pub, would order something like a lemonade shandy and hack away happily at the Cheddar. At such times my grandmother became concentrated and dangerous. She would scythe through the saloon bar into the public, seize the plate of cheese and take it into the kitchen. 'Hungry sod,' she would mutter furiously. 'I'm not taking it out again till he's gorn.'

It was things like this that I didn't understand, as a child. I simply absorbed it all.

I spent much of my early life at the pub. My grandmother was a babysitter, of sorts. This was a time when adults led their own lives, rather than fretting around those of their offspring, and my parents went out a great deal. My father was a racing man, which meant thrice-weekly nights at the dogs (to which I was sometimes taken); also, not infrequently, the horses. In those days of the 1970s, big races like the Derby were run during the week. My grandmother would pick me up from school in her dark blue MG, which she drove dashingly and badly, with much angry wobbling of the gearstick. Her face would be half-done for the evening, her hair in curlers under a Jacqmar headscarf. If I found her waiting for me, she would be peering in the car mirror, quite possibly with tweezers in her hand. She looked superbly incongruous, sitting there among the neat spillages of uniformed pupils. She would have watched the racing on television, and had her bets, and remembered the Derbies she had seen 'before the war', watching from a bus in the centre of the course; and that, elliptically, is what we talked about on the drive to the pub. 'What did you do at school today?' was not in her repertoire of remarks. Unlike her daughter, my mother, she had no interest in even simulating an interest in the world of childhood, and I completely accepted this.

I felt a sweet apprehension as the MG rounded the bend in the long village road and I saw the inn sign, swinging high in the air on its gallows. Even then, I realised something about pubs: that they were home but not quite home. They were as dear and familiar to people as home, but they were also the place where people escaped from home.

The pub, situated in the rural Home Counties, was very small, very old and extremely pretty. To me it seemed enchanted. It had a trimly thatched roof, shuttered windows, white walls with a wobbly grid of black beams – the works – and its classic English *chiaroscuro* was splashed, in summer, with profusions of colour from hanging baskets that dripped with water (the principle of 'a *good* drink' extending to the flowers). It looked like an artist's sketch upon the landscape, framed by hills that hovered calmly in the distance. Across the narrow road, seeming at times to overspill its bounds, was a towering tangle of ancient woodland. The village was set on a steep incline, and so too therefore was the pub. Everything sloped, giving a tumbledown feeling to the stone-paved courtyard outside the front doors, which was set with a couple of tables. The large garden, always called 'the orchard', rolled sharply away towards fields that my memory sees as infinite.

So: a near-perfect specimen of the country pub. Like all the best pubs, however, it was completely un-twee. Held within its quaint exterior was a red-lit world of sophistication, sentiment, vulgarity and warmth. This came partly from its communion with my grandmother, who was not quaint in any way, and not good with the kind of person who asked jovial, pedantic questions about her 'ales' or was liable to use the word 'hostelry'. It was easier to imagine her serving Reg Kray than, say, a group of map-clutching ramblers (although these did occasionally come in, fresh from the ancient woodland in which I once had a close escape from a pervert. I was shaken but not shocked: my pub training).

Indeed she was, on the face of it, an unlikely landlady for this dear little place, which looked like the home of a traditional blacksmith, or of a countrywoman with geese and a herb garden. With her Harrods hair and gold ankle chain, my grandmother should have been as out of place as a showgirl running a WI cake stall. Yet somehow this was not the case. For a start she was never out of place, in the sense that she never worried about such things (she would have remained entirely herself if transported to Holloway jail or Buckingham Palace). And then, she imprinted her own personality upon the pub: such was her power as a landlady. She bestrode the bars, she infused them with her style. At the same time, again like a great landlady, she knew what not to do. She respected the pub, rather as she would have respected a man. She allowed it its natural vigour. For all that it looked so picturesque, it had a kind of steel in its soul: it too rejected the implications of its appearance. Georgie Pillson might have turned up to paint it, but he would soon have fled in terror. It was rooted in a village of farmers and butchers, it was a mere couple of miles from a town of committed gin-drinkers and adulterers; in sum, it was robust and real and belonged to life, not to an image of what a pub should be. It had stood for almost 550 years, and age had given it complete assurance. It had the almost sunken air of a place that knew exactly why it was there; and never more so, I am fairly sure, than in the years of its alliance with my grandmother.

As was obvious from its roadside position, it had originally been an inn. An old photograph shows a sign offering 'stabling'. Such was its antiquity (it had listed status) that treasures had been unearthed from it – a painting was removed to the National Gallery. Typically, my grandmother's recollection of this was vague. So too when historical societies visited the pub. The members would enter in a polite, bright-eyed, expectant mass of tweed jackets and dirndl skirts, smiling blindly into the dour faces of farmers, then gather in front of a plaque in the saloon bar. They would repeat in obedient whispers the words that I knew by heart, that the inn was an 'ancient monument' built during the Wars of the Roses, that some of its beams were original, etc., etc. If my grandmother chanced to float through the bar, they would pounce, asking pleasant, historian-type questions that she could not answer (she would have breezed over this, 'ah well, ma'am/sir, nobody really knows…' but she never liked being at a loss). Not that she was indifferent to the provenance of the pub. She was fiercely proud of everything about it. She simply saw things, including the past, in her own way.

Her history was enough for her, and the past, to her, meant pubs. She was born, a century ago now, in Paddington Green. Her father, who always worked in pubs, later ran his own establishment. So too did some of her relations and most of her friends, 'old Jim and Hilda at the Star and Garter', or 'old Bernard at the White Horse', or whoever it might be. She spoke as if everybody, me aged six included, should know who they were: as if publicans were a famed species. On a drive she would always peer at any pubs she passed, rather as if they were her personal responsibility. She even gravitated to a pub inside Harrods, the Green Man, a delightful little anomalous dark hole in the basement beside the men's hairdresser, where she would sit at her observational post, feet covered in green and gold bags, and drink a schooner of dry sherry. Long gone, of course.

Yes, she saw the whole of life through that particular prism, which was in fact a large and enlightened one. Pubs, to her, were not just a job. They were more like a calling. A way of being. A touchstone, a symbol. There was nothing mystical or delusional about her love of them; she knew perfectly well that they could be tawdry or nasty or criminally dull. But her greatness as a landlady came from the fact that she believed, with a true faith, that a proper pub was a beautiful thing.

At the time I am describing she had run her own pub for some twenty-five years. It was her remarkable creation, her life's work. Yet she defined herself, or so it seemed to me, by her father's pub: the 'old pub'. This was the place that had shaped her, to the point where she and pubs became as one, and the rhythms of pub life as instinctive to her as breathing. The landlady was not merely a persona that she assumed. From an early age it had become indivisible from her nature.

Had her formative years not been spent in a pub, had she been the daughter of a solicitor (for instance), she would obviously have grown up different. How, it is impossible to say. It is also absolutely impossible to imagine. A housewife?

An office worker? How would those lives have encompassed her? Without the demanding refuge of the bar, what would have happened to that bohemian soul of hers? I think that she would always, somehow, have displayed the true pub qualities: the toughness, the bonhomie, the spaciousness of spirit, the commonplace daily courage, the refusal to judge alongside the implicit steadfast standards. But because of her environment, these qualities were set free and writ large.

I have no idea if she herself thought this way. She was wonderfully free of introspection. This was key to her character. She did not analyse, and she did not dwell on things. Her memories of the 'old pub' were not nostalgic, exactly; rather they helped her to keep the past fused with the present.

Above all – and again this was what pubs required – she had a tireless ability to push her personality outwards. She did this willingly, with an effort that was also an instinct, even after her life at the pub was over. It was extraordinary, really. Nobody who met her was resistant to her. What a force she was! Aged ninety she would prowl through our local Morrisons, a small, powerful figure in her loose leopard-print coat (bought in Beauchamp Place in the late 1970s), slow but full of restless energy, fingers twitching with the old irritable urges to shape her surroundings, bestowing herself upon the boys who sullenly stacked apples and peaches ('find us a few nice ones'), cascading a glamour through the aisles that was utterly indestructible. One of the reasons why I am bored to death by the modern obsession with female ageing is that I grew up watching my grandmother, not so much defying her years as completely untroubled by them, apparently believing that whatever age she was at the time was the right age to be. Actually she is the reason why I am bored by all modern female hang-ups, including the fact of being female itself. 'Always thought I was slightly better than a man,' was one of her throwaway remarks. She was the most confident woman I have ever known, Lawrence's Anna Brangwen transported to a faintly louche and gleaming saloon bar. And she could cut away at self-importance with one good-natured sweep. My mother and I once took her to a London restaurant, much cooed over in magazines, run by a deeply silly 'legend' of whom most customers professed to be in awe. 'Got a nice lobster, duck?' asked my grandmother amiably, one host to another, as the famed maître d' loomed over our table.

She never needed to self-mythologise in that way. Her own legend had arisen quite naturally and she let the customers bolster it, rather than doing so herself. Nor, despite her flamboyance, did she display vulgarity or gaudiness, in the manner of the cliché landlady (if such a person actually exists). She always held something in reserve. In style and demeanour she most resembled an old-style theatrical performer, a semi-retired Coral Browne or Hermione Gingold. 'She should have been on the stage,' my father used to say. In fact that wasn't quite right. She had her stage already.

For a pub is a theatre in which people are playing themselves. It is a public house, after all. This is a deceptively simple title, a perfect definition of the paradox that one is at home, but also escaping from home. One is relaxed, but bracingly relaxed. The proper pub is a place where people become their public selves, rather than their private; the division of personality that makes life a business worth engaging with, and that has all but disappeared into the deadly vortex of the smartphone.

My grandmother, who had a lot of self to play, played herself better than most. She learned to do so at such a young age that it became innate; but she also saw it as a duty, and in her staunch, frivolous way she believed in duty. Put on a show, be fun, drown your sorrows, don't be a bloody bore. Even as a child I understood, and sought to keep up a show in her presence. 'Chin up,' she would say, to a tale of playground perfidy; it was the pub code, which she embodied and I revered.

Of course there were dead times in her pub: it wasn't the Algonquin (although imagine how boring that must sometimes have been! – all that relentless wit). And of course there were lots of bores in her pub. If they clearly couldn't help it, then that was acceptable, one had compassion, but she once actually barred a cocky, creepy man for being, as she put it, 'a nuisance to people' – in other words a bore. He didn't mind at all, and was back within the week, striving and failing to be bearable; even he subscribed to the code. For my grandmother, meanwhile, the notion that one would go into a public arena and behave as one did in private – slumping, subsiding, staring at a screen – was as inconceivable to her as showing the world a face untouched by the sainted Lauder.

In those days there were licensing hours, which placed a limit upon pleasure in a very English way. The twice-daily closing and opening was again, of course, exactly like theatre: lights up and down, make-up on and off, matinée and evening. Also theatrical was the separation between the bars, 'out front', and the living quarters: backstage. I was beguiled by this division between two worlds, this mystery, marked so simply by the discreet wooden door in the far corner of the saloon bar, which opened on to my grandmother's sitting room. The tiny dark space in front of that door was the dead zone of the pub. It puts me in mind now of one of those music hall Sickerts, in which both performer and audience are visible. In one direction were bursts of vital, indiscriminate sound; in the other, an occluded humming near-silence.

I lived mostly backstage, during opening hours at least. My grandmother, supremely broadminded but at the same time absolutist in her diktats, was very much against children in pubs. If it was cold then they sat in the car and their parents took them a bottle of R. White's with a straw in it (some people, much despised, would stipulate the colour of the straw). If it was warm then they had the vast 'orchard' at their disposal, separated from the car park by a small stone wall, a downward-sloping expanse of lawn with a swing and climbing frame at the bottom. At the top of the hill was a flat plain, laid out with tables and chairs made of white wrought iron (regularly painted, like tennis shoes). This sunlit outpost was for people who were not really of the pub: healthful types like cyclists, wholesome types who liked views, couples for whom the view formed a third party, and families. If parents tried to bring their children into the bar my grandmother was quite capable of requesting that they put them out, like dogs – although dogs were very welcome. A complaint about the child-ejection policy was once made by an aggrieved father, but she was unrepentant. She was nice to children, but always in that vague, smiling, drifting way of hers, which signified an essential lack of interest. She could not accept the pub as anything but a place for adults, preferably men, although not the kind of man who wanted to drink with a three-year-old.

I loved the orchard, not when customers were cluttering up the tables with their splayed bags of crisps and fingerprint-smeared bottles, but when it belonged to me alone. Oh, the three o'clock summer light of that garden. Running at speed from the flat plain at the top; I can still feel the sudden sharp dip in the earth, the 'look no hands' sense of the hill taking me down with it. Of course I remember it as bigger than it was. In later years I was honestly amazed to see that the space, though very large, was a visibly contained rectangle. Not that this changes at all the memories of hurtling towards the apple trees that gave the orchard its name, and then into the beginning of wildness, where the grass was not mowed and the early summer cow parsley reached my waist. It was a dreamscape, in which the pub became a magical house (my house) and the sloping lawn an unchanging, buttercup-studded paradise; I stood on the swing and pushed higher and higher to face the ancient woodland, lay in the grass and searched passionately for four-leaf clovers, told the time with dandelion clocks, absorbed myself in the present-tense eternity of childhood. This was when I was happiest at the pub, which is odd because I was doing things that I could do at home, so what made them so memorable? It was because afternoons in the orchard were not like ordinary afternoons. They were a parenthesis. Time was suspended but stolen; precious in a way that did not touch me, but that I recognised. Waiting at the top of the hill was the smoky *palais* that only masqueraded as an English country cottage, that winked slyly at the brilliance of its own disguise, that compelled me equally, and that made the orchard seem peculiarly prelapsarian: even then, I knew this.

When the stage was empty, I got to know almost every corner of it. In the early mornings – before school, or during holidays – I would go, as one entering a secret chamber, through the door into the saloon. Straight ahead, down a shallow step, insultingly adept at tripping up drunkards, was the door into the public bar. All was dark brick, fretted with heavy wood, humming with silence.

The saloon and public bars were almost identical, except in atmosphere, although at that hour atmosphere was in hibernation. One knew that it had been there, and that it would be there again, but for the moment it was holding itself in abeyance. The air was grey and uncertain, ghostly with dust, streaked with lines of smoke. A thin trail of day eased its way between the curtains; the dust motes danced where it fell, and a crazy solar system of circles gleamed on the tabletops. A brisk clearing-up would have taken place the night before but a few things lingered, like clues in a bad detective story: a couple of sodden beer mats (one perhaps with a phone number on it, never to be rung), a last defiant Embassy stubbed into the ashtrays lined up for cleaning, a shifty glass oiled with whisky dregs.

The bars were tiny. One was more aware of this, oddly, when they were empty. It seemed quite impossible that so much life could fit into them. The ceilings were low – the heads of tall men always seemed to be negotiating with them – and the spaces between the beams were dirty-mellow with nicotine. Seats were pushed up hard against the walls: black settles from the 'old pub', with backs curved like shields and smooth slippery seats. A pub is never truly light inside – there is always that interplay of glint and dusk – but on sunny days, with the old sash windows behind them, the settles shone like the coats of young Labradors.

The shimmering look of those early pub mornings, poised between hush and promise… only memory can reproduce their nuances of shadow and clarity, infinite in their imprecision. And memory also holds the hovering quiet, broken by the tentative creaks of the floor, the drip of tap or optic. It holds textures: the beams solid and splintery to the touch, and the stone surrounds of the giant fireplaces rough and cold. Hidden behind these surrounds were shallow seats, ledges built into the stone. These were a great delight to me, although (and despite my obsession with kings and queens) I never pondered the fact that people must have sat on those ledges since the time of Henry VI. The history of the pub was a feather in its cap, no question, but the historical-society view was somehow irrelevant. The plaque in the saloon bar described the pub as an ancient monument. For sure it never behaved like one. Like my grandmother, it revered its past but absorbed it into the present; in a good pub, the accretions of memory are palpable, but all time is the same.

At the heart of the pub was the bar itself. The coppery counter, which formed an L-shape, faced the public bar and looked sideways on to the saloon. Behind it, in the pungent little space that would barely hold three people, I would serve pretend rounds and put my nose – later my appalled tongue – to the different drinks. Here, I knew, was the alchemist's headquarters. I can remember every detail: to my right hand were two beer pumps – Tankard and (far less popular) Trophy – plus a pump of Heineken, with plastic trays beneath that constantly overflowed. When the barrel was changed the pump was as lively and spiteful as a tiger cub, the first pint an explosion of what looked like whisked egg white. Beside the pumps was a wrench for removing bottle tops, above a rusty tin box into which they theoretically fell; there was also a pedal bin, but that too was a hit-and-miss receptacle. When the pub got busy, and the banknotes were waved and waggled by a towering criss-cross of hands (always male hands), nothing mattered except getting people served: rubbish could pile up at one's feet, cigarettes could shrivel to grey tubes, the sink could block, the very world could end, but old Mick would get his large Bell's, 'When you're ready, duck...' The sink was at the front of the bar, beneath the counter. In the course of an evening it became murky with slops, and the water level rose to dark and alarming levels. The square of dark red carpet was soaked with spills and scored with ash: everybody smoked behind the bar. Occasionally a customer would hold up a glass to show a drink flecked with grey-black. 'Cheeky sod,' my grandmother would say, meaning that she disliked having been caught out. On the lower shelves were rows of bottles: mixers – R. White's, Britvic, Schweppes (*you know who*); Guinness (*is good for you*), Double Diamond (*works wonders*), Mackeson, Bass; Cherry B, Babycham, Moussec; and at the bottom, dusty and terrible as bottles of strychnine, the fearsomely strong White Shield and barley wine.

The shelf beside the till was always damp and slimy. Here were the lemons, oozing pips on their little chopping board; the sticky cherries speared with cocktail sticks; the pads and pens; the silver drink measures, which my grandmother thought embarrassingly inadequate and basically ignored – also more arcane items, Angostura, Lea & Perrin's – and what would now be item-in-chief, a sole bottle of white wine, which then held almost no interest at all. Wine was what one drank, possibly, with dinner. One female customer, splendid as a shire horse, would ask for what she called a 'double wine', meaning two glasses poured into another, much larger glass; otherwise the scented Liebfraumilch in its flowery bottle took its humble place beside the Stone's Ginger Wine (for a whisky mac) and the Bols Advocaat (for a monstrous concoction known as a 'snowball', in which the thick yellow stuff was puffed up with lemonade like a soufflé). There was also Rose's lime juice, which might be dashed into lager for a cost of 5p, although one customer found this a bridge too far. 'A pint of lager,' he would say, and pause. '*With* some lime,' meaning as an afterthought, an adjunct, for which payment was unnecessary.

At eye level were the bottles of spirits, hanging upside-down in front of a mirror. The prices stuck untidily on the optics – 50p, 65p – were changed after every Budget: always a black day, on which the plate of cheese was temporarily withdrawn ('can't afford to do that now'). On the glass shelf above was another level of bottles, rarely opened although even more gorgeous and glittering, their contents the colours of jewels: curaçao, grenadine, Drambuie, Green Goddess, Parfait Amour, and crème de menthe ('tart's drink'), for which ice had to be crushed in a little mincer. Cigarettes were stacked in rows, and the cellophane-shiny colours of Dunhill, Benson & Hedges and St Moritz gleamed beneath the golden bell for calling time. On the high shelves around the front of the bar were the inverted tumblers and goblets (so demure in size compared with those of today), which my grandmother polished every morning in her carelessly capable way. Pint glasses swung from hooks in the shelves, catching stray diamonds of light. A couple of white drying-up cloths flopped across the counter in an attitude of exhaustion. In the dark sink below, a gathering of what had once been lemon slices lay around the plughole in a shallow pool of spume.

At this hour, the bar was drained of colour, its sheen dimmed, tired and unlovely like the morning bodies of the people it had served the night before. Yet throughout the day it would take on warmth and light, to the point when – to those who could not see the overflowing beer trays, the sink full of foaming water, the litter of bottle tops and fag ends – it became luminous, configurative, the gleam of glass and mirror and electricity so much refracted as to fuse into an absolute of light. It was a shining cave of plenitude, a lucent vision that a child might dream, that offered a promise and haven of the most adult kind.

In the public bar was the door to the cellar. From the outside this looked like a thatched wooden barn attached to the pub, sloping downwards along with everything else. The giveaway was the low double-door, opened when the barrels were changed (a sadistically noisy business, like an industrial blood transfusion). The 'barn' stood above the cellar proper. It had been built by the brewery in the 1950s, when my grandmother was not long at the pub, and its chilly interior was like a large cell. It contained my grandmother's accounts, one of the few things that could make her panic; stacked boxes of Walker's crisps, behind which I once surprised a semi-dressed couple; and the ice machine. Ice: what a tyrant. Perfectly nice people became touchy if they felt that their drink did not contain its full quota (there were also those who, fearing any weakening of the drink, would sternly forbid its presence). Busy evenings meant the frequent crowd-surfing passage of empty ice buckets to whoever was willing to fill them – sometimes a good-natured customer – and every night held the unspoken prayer that nothing should go wrong with the ice machine. I remember its arrival, the wonder of all those cubes. Before that there had been a constant filling and disgorging of ice trays. As a girl, my grandmother had wheeled a pram every day containing a miniature glacier (from the local tannery) back to her father's pub, where it would be chipped at like a sculpture.

The cellar at the old pub – paradoxically, a much newer establishment – had run underneath the whole ground floor, and served as an air-raid shelter during the war. At my grandmother's pub, the cellar proper was a true medieval oubliette, big enough for nothing but barrels, a grey hollow reached by a twisting staircase of rock-like steps. Before the barn was built, one opened the cellar door and was launched straight at the staircase; enormously dangerous, although nobody thought that way. In the early years of the twentieth century, jugs of beer were filled straight from the barrels. Down and up went the bartender, down and up the treacherous grey steps.

What with the wildly thrumming barrels and the juddering whirr of the ice machine, the cellar always seemed to shake, and it smelled fiercely of beer and cold stone. Smell, of course... the pub in the mornings had an acid, weary smell that I can still conjure, bred from the coupling of booze and smoke: a smell of aftermath. Cleaning was not the answer, what was needed was more of the same – a fresh new pint pulled, a pristine cigarette sparked up, the hair of the dog principle as a guide to life; nevertheless, by 8.30 a.m. the beer-fag miasma was penetrated by a powerful stream of disinfectant from a tin bucket propped against the door of the Gents' in the public bar. Within I could hear Mrs Brennan, the cleaner, banging around with her mop, singing wheezily, 'yew were meant, for me... *and* ay was meant, for yew!' She had hair permed to a crisp and an Embassy glued to her bright pink lower lip. From the open door came another smell, unspeakable, winding its way through the

Jeyes fluid. I was nervous of the Gents', and never once went inside it. The Ladies' I loved: a lush Camay-scented cave.

Later Mrs Brennan would polish the dark red tiles around the edge of the floors, then tackle the carpets. Every morning they were newly dank, swiped with commas of ash – some of it Mrs Brennan's own – and posing the intractable problem of the sodden strip beside my grandmother's stool, where whisky and cleaning fluid fought for supremacy, and an unhappy mingling of the two ensued. It was not until the evening, when my grandmother was re-established in her pitch, that her rich cosmetic scent took possession of the air; although she would then recreate the original problem by throwing yet more whisky onto the floor.

The kind, industrious Mrs Brennan (who in the 1980s would become the only worker in a family of five) lived in one of the council houses along the road, beyond the woodland and towards the town, by which point the village was no longer picturesque but instead one of those hard, flat, transitional areas – neither country nor urban – in which England abounds although no notice is paid to them. The houses brandished TV aerials like antlers, and their pale lawns were decorated with ornamental lions and the like. A couple of men from these houses got a bus to the pub in the early evenings (there was a stop directly opposite, carved bathetically into the ancient woodland). In the public bar they would commune with other customers, a sparse assortment at this time, in the sidelong, semaphore way of men who would normally have nothing to say to each other: 'all right, boy?'; 'what you having then, mate?'; the brusque, courteous democracy of the true pub. Now this would be called 'community'. Then, again, nobody thought that way. They simply did things.

By around nine in the morning, the day had lurched further forwards away from me, into normality, as an erratic timpani of rattling and clinking struck up to punctuate Mrs Brennan's banging and singing. This was 'bottling up': the boy who did the garden – silent of person, rampantly noisy in his work – hurling the empties into crates, tipping rubbish into sacks. Soon the boy would be seated in the saloon, still silent beneath his abundance of sulky dark hair, eating the enormous savoury breakfast provided by my grandmother (she adored hungry young men) while Mrs Brennan smiled indulgently ('bless him') from her stool at the bar, blowing on her coffee cup in between puffs on her fag. The pair were positioned like customers, but they were a facsimile only, understudies on a stage that had lost its half-lit mystery but was not yet transfigured by performance. I had no interest in the pub at that point. As was my privilege, of which even then I was aware, I retreated backstage into the squashy warm embrace of my grandmother's sitting room.

In this other world, all was comfort and plenitude. There was nothing 'cosy' about it, in the peculiarly English sense of the word; it was not a room in which to 'curl up' and read detective stories or listen to *Book at Bedtime*: there was still that bite of worldliness in the air. But the tiny space was as warm as cashmere, the sofa was the softest I have ever sat on and the armchair, my grandmother's seat, reclined with a prolonged luxurious thud. Beside it was the old-fashioned dial telephone – the receiver grimed

24

with foundation cream – which she answered in a strange voice ('Hay-lloh-oo-agh?') at the extreme edge of her low, full, croaky, part-London, part-exotic, part-theatrical vibrato. A carved oak cabinet from the old pub held decanters of heavy cut glass, filled with the liquid toffee of good whisky and brandy; on the marble tables were silver cigarette boxes, silver dishes glistening with Quality Street and After Eights. Wedged somewhere inside the sofa were the two chihuahua dogs, whom I loved with a near-unbearable passion. One, Tom, was pale and poignantly pretty. The other, Ted, was brown, fat-necked and sickly, with beseeching eyes; my grandmother had chosen him because she knew that nobody would want him (she was tough, but not about things like that). They sat either side of me, compact little heated armrests with soft bug ears aloft, while I looked through *Harpers & Queen* and listened, in uncomprehending and slightly wary pleasure, to the elliptical conversations going on in the kitchen.

This was a doll-size strip of room which, like the bar, could fit no more than three people. Even then it seemed to smell of the past, of lard and Brillo and a robust disdain for food hygiene. It had a larder hung with fly papers, a venomous old oven and a high window through which (such was the downward tilt of everything) one could watch passing pedestrian feet. The air was hazy with frying-pan heat – my grandmother believed in breakfast – and the back door was usually left open. It led to an alley, reeking of old beer, among which the flicking tail of a rat might be seen.

The kitchen was where my grandmother spent the early

mornings. The first cup of tea came out of a Teasmade by the side of her bed, then she padded downstairs with a dog under each arm. She stood and sipped and talked without cease to her cousin, Irene, a sharp little red-haired woman who lived with her at the pub. My grandmother was a divorcée of many years standing; Irene was a widow: the arrangement must have had a kind of inevitability about it. Irene and her husband, Stan, had also run a pub, so were family in both senses. They had married at the end of the war, when he was flush and flash with the profits of buying whisky from GIs then selling it to customers (according to my father, who always knew these things, the 'unkoshered' cash was kept in a secret drawer in Irene's dressing table). I later learned that Stan had paid serious court to my grandmother before moving on to Irene. This was never mentioned. Somehow it was clear that it was also never forgotten: the relationship between the two women was composed of an unbreakable bond of jealousy and solidarity. At the time, this was again something that I drank in without understanding.

To the muted sound of Radio 2 the two women would bustle about the kitchen, getting in each other's way, drinking tea and trying to fit too-thick slices of bread under the grill (my grandmother's toast always had black edges, like mourning cards). They wore ageing silky wraps smeared with make-up, and lumpy hairnets over tight-screwed curlers. Naturally they smoked. There were cigarette burns on every surface; the satin quilt on my grandmother's bed was pierced with little brown-black holes. In her view tipped cigarettes were not the real thing, and she smoked the Player's Navy Cut of her youth. However, Irene, in the interests of health, had recently moved on to the menthol brand of St Moritz, which remained in her mouth when she was coating her head in Nice'n Easy auburn dye.

Sometimes my grandmother would sit on a stool in an untypically dramatic pose, holding a flannel to her forehead. She was never able to tolerate hangovers and, although these did not happen often, they were the focus of the morning. 'There *isn't* a cure,' she would say, irritably, when Irene proffered an Alka-Seltzer fizzing in a glass, or a Bloody Mary dense with celery salt. 'Take it away, Rene. There *isn't* a cure.'

The two women talked in a way that I thought of as adult, as if in code. The volume dropped away at salient moments. Their tone was snappish yet intimate. Long silences brimmed with meaning. Their subject matter was almost entirely the customers; they were not the kind of women who openly discussed their own lives. They knew everything about each other but colluded in concealment. For instance my grandmother, who could be almost angrily loyal, went along with the rehabilitation of the spiv Stan as 'a businessman'. Irene, who both respected and resented my grandmother's essential decency, was more complex in her self-restraint; she was a repository of unpredictable emotions, which flicked out with the controlled suddenness of a snake's tongue. She was in fact what my grandmother, in another context, would have called 'an old tab' (tabby cat = catty), but because of who she was this was accepted.

During their conversations they fell into roles. Invariably Irene made the opening move, a small flare of spite (it was tacitly acknowledged that this was her skill), which my grandmother would then modify, contradict or enlarge upon.

'Ron brought that little tart in here again, then?'

'Oh well, Rene.' I sensed one of my grandmother's worldly shrugs. 'You know a girl can wrap a man like that round her finger. You know what a girl can do, if she's got a bit of sense.'

There was a pause, while Irene turned bacon rashers with a quick, jabbing fork. Then she said:

'He's a silly sod, though, eh?'

'Oh, proper soppy.'

When she pronounced judgments of that kind, my grandmother's tone was fatalistic, as if she were stating something obvious to all but the insane; also something that could never be changed, an immutable fact of life. She revered men but held them in contempt for their sexual susceptibility, which in those days they were more flagrant and fearless about. She regarded women as superior in sense, and liked their company, but she always put men first. They were the ones, the people who mattered. There was no gainsaying it. At the same time she would raise a metaphorical eyebrow, as if to say, *Ridiculous, isn't it?*

While she would always pronounce 'you've got to have a man' (if for instance my father dealt with her VAT), she was living proof of her belief that a woman, 'if she's got a bit of something about her', could do whatever she chose. The pub was her creation, with Irene as chief handmaiden and a procession of barmaids as industrious train-bearers. It was a place made by women. My grandmother, one might say, was a feminist before the age of feminism (as were most of her close friends). If I had told her this she would have understood the idea, in so far as she cared to do so, but at the same time have dismissed it as irrelevant. 'Um... well, I ran a good house, I suppose.' She had done what she did and that was that.

And she had done it, primarily, for men, because it was they who truly needed pubs. Women merely liked them. Years later she remarked to me that, in the early days of her landlady life, a few female customers would come and drink in the saloon bar unaccompanied by men – then extremely unusual – and had told her that they felt comfortable enough to do this because the pub was run by women. I responded with some modern stuff of the kind that my grandmother never dealt in. 'Um... they were on the pick-up, I suppose.'

She was a mass of apparent contradictions, but the strength of her personality always resolved them. And I always knew what she meant. As a child I didn't literally know, but I grasped that she was dealing in ambiguities and I trusted her to pull it off. I was mesmerised by her, really. Children are attracted to certainty, and she possessed this quality more than anybody I have ever met. One day she and Irene were in the kitchen examining a photo of a taut-faced Marlene Dietrich in the paper. 'Had a good lift, she has,' Irene said. 'Be nice to have that done, eh, Vi?' My grandmother never responded to cattiness.

'Never thought there was much wrong with my old kisser,' she said blithely.

Those kitchen conversations were tremulously beautiful to my ears. I understood very little, and indeed still wouldn't understand everything. I simply loved the rhythms, the measured ripples of female wisdom. I loved the way in which character was both distilled – 'well, he's an old boy, isn't he' – and left mysterious. Although I am incapable of that idiom, it is ingrained in me: variations on my grandmother's phrases still dance through my head whenever the modern world threatens to overwhelm with its lunacies, and put it firmly back in its place.

So who were the people that these two women discussed, in that way of theirs, which was not exactly gossipy, more as if they had made a long study of human nature and sought daily, regretful, satisfying confirmation of their worst conclusions? The pub customers divided roughly into three sets, overlapping of course (including in their sexual encounters), of whom the third set provided the most conversational material.

The first set comprised the local country people, who had used the pub for generations. Even as a child I felt comfortable with them, they were so comfortable with themselves and with their reason for being alive. (I feel the same way now. 'Done any writing lately, girl? Good on you.') They were ribald, wholesome even in their lusts, and they could drink anybody under the table ('oh we had bushels of drink'). Like the Starkadders they burned with an extraordinary life force; the huge laughter of the men threw not just their heads, but their chest and shoulders, up towards the beams. They were all in some way related to each other – the odder, Urk-like members of the dynasties tended to drink elsewhere; pubs call with animal accuracy to their own kind – and between them they owned thousands of acres. They were also clever with money: skilled manipulators of EEC regulations, expert gamblers and shrewd card players. Essentially they were all farmers, but one of them was also a successful amateur jockey, while another was a butcher who would call my grandmother behind the counter ('Come on, Miss Vi!') to choose from his cuts of meat. Their eccentricity was unforced. Stories abounded of behaviour that was quite normal to them but left outsiders with mouths agape. For example during a dinner at one of their rambling, roistering houses, a guest who went upstairs in search of a loo was confronted by a dead pig in the bath. They were, ostensibly, completely different from my grandmother; yet in vitality, in extroversion, in their disdain for all that was circumscribed and petty, the country people resembled her closely. They were made on the grand scale and they filled the pub in every sense. Many years later I was approached by one of them around the paddock at Royal Ascot, where amid all the flummery he had been examining the horseflesh with an experienced eye. 'Vi's granddaughter,' he said, as one who perceived not just my name badge but my true identity, which in some inexplicable way made my day.

The second set of customers was 'passing trade'. It was a running joke that when anyone unfamiliar walked in, the entire place stopped dead, as if everybody were playing statues. It was part of the pub's charm, this clubbishness, although there were inevitably those who disliked it. One night a young man strode into the saloon bar wearing a black leather jacket, looking, as he thought, rather cool and sexy. 'Oo'er,' I heard my grandmother say, in one of her famous stage whispers. '*Saucebox.*' And only God could help the courting couples who came for a nice quiet romantic drink. 'Who are those dozy young buggers in that inglenook, Vi?' one of the farmers would say (there was a general belief that remarks made in the public bar could not be heard in the saloon). 'Not bought a bloody drink all night.' The farmers missed nothing. 'Well, I say that, about two hours ago he ordered a *half…*' Halves were things that you poured on top of five-eighths-empty pints ('Stick us a half in there,' meaning fill it up again). Bought specifically, they were suspect.

Occasionally what appeared to be passing trade was in fact somebody known to my grandmother, a person from the past who had come in to spring a lovely surprise upon her. Sometimes (not terribly often) she was indeed pleased to see whoever it was. Sometimes she had no idea who they were, a fact that she concealed with a fairly impressive faked ecstasy, before hissing for aid in one of her stage whispers. Sometimes she did not want to see the person at all. On one particular evening an old suitor came sidling into the pub, thinking to delight her with his presence; those who heard it never forgot the precise tone of her *sotto voce* 'oh fuck' as the aged dandy pranced towards her. When he left, a couple of hours later, he reversed his car into that of another customer and returned, laughing in an ill-judged way. 'No, no, it's quite all right,' he said, to the seething car owner, 'I'm a *friend of Vi's.*'

He was half-cut, of course, although probably the man whose car he pranged would have been too. Most people drove home over the limit. When the breathalyser was introduced, my grandmother – sensing trouble – abandoned her usual sports cars and bought a large Humber with which to transport customers to and from their homes. Then it became clear that not many of them were worried about the breathalyser. In the main they lived very close to the pub and could make the journey on autopilot. Nobody ever caused an accident, although my father, who regularly stopped for a drink on his way home from London, and occasionally became what he called 'inveigled', did once drive over a roundabout (as opposed to around it) and in so doing uprooted a sapling tree, which he found the next day underneath his Jensen Interceptor. He told the callow policeman who tracked him down that he had swerved to avoid a cat, and got away with it. This was not good, not to be condoned. But it was how it was.

Prominent among the drink-drivers were the third set of customers, who came from the nearby town. On the whole they were well off, although not idle rich; even the retired among them carried an air of former industry, a knowledge of shop floors and ends that had not met. Most were very generous. Those who displayed the merest hint of carefulness were at the mercy of the farmers: 'About time you bought a bloody drink, isn't it, boy? You've been guzzling away...' Some of the townspeople were publicans: always favoured. Some were 'in the car trade', or 'the building trade'. One was 'in sacks', a profitable industry, and would pay for a single light ale with a £20 note. One was 'in tax', and accordingly mistrusted. Another was 'in antiques', attended by a succession of brightly deferential young men with an eye to his Louis Quinze (much kitchen conversation about the fact that he dared not come out to his mother). Another, who inherited lot of money, would come in night after night, buying tumultuous rounds with much display of Rolex and American Express (both gold), until he had realised his subliminal aim of spending his way back to zero. He continued to haunt the pub, meekly accepting drinks, offering in return the provincial myth of his rise and fall. Yet another, a pleasant middle-aged man in slacks and steel-rimmed specs, the very image of reliable middle management, learned one day that his wife was having an affair, drove off in his Volvo and shot himself.

Within this loose category of customer were subsets: for instance a gang of three who stood in the saloon bar (odd, for men), drank from special silver tankards (odd and twee), and were later revealed to be a homosexual couple plus an indeterminate other. A more elusive and glamorous group, adored by my grandmother, who had known them since they were 'boys', turned up on select Sundays in tight-belted denim (containing the loosening gut) and sports cars (roof down as soon as the temperature rose above fifteen degrees). For a time one of them drove a Ferrari, clearly the only thing on his mind and, he clearly hoped, on everybody else's. They liked to congregate in the courtyard outside the front of the pub, where they could continue to stare lovingly at their low-slung vehicles; they carried an air of Silverstone and

Marbella, and had school-of-Rod-Stewart girlfriends with whom they occasionally embarked upon slightly hysterical, short-lived marriages. They were also, essentially, sweet-natured and innocent; when I think of them now, I sense a lurking collection of Dinky cars.

The older, more venerable townspeople came in the mornings. The men dressed like golf club presidents, or aldermen (one of them was indeed the local mayor). Their women were often very elegant. Hair lacquered and backcombed, as if by precision engineering. Stockings that were obviously stockings. False nails that occasionally fell into an ashtray. I recall one such woman, perched on a stool in the saloon bar, who had the high grey chignon of a former ballerina and the elocution of a Rank starlet; I was too young to understand how she could bear the company of a big, bluff, comfortable man whose navy blazer smelled of whisky and was scattered with dandruff, glinting festively in the pub daylight. They were not married. They lived in sin, in suburbia. Years later, when the man was dying, he severed every tie with his exquisite mistress and returned to his wife for absolution, whereupon the mistress crumbled with dramatic speed and took on the aspect of a bag lady.

Dominant within the third set of customers were the youngish, urban regulars who arrived most evenings after nine o'clock. They looked very different from thirtysomethings nowadays, none of that aping of extreme youth. They all, men and women, had a trim sitcom smartness. The women wore neat blouses slung with gold chains; some of the men also wore gold chains – what my grandmother would have called 'big 'uns'. Whereas the farmers drank beer and whisky, these people drank Bacardi and Coke, brandy and soda, or most popularly gin and slimline (gin when it was the norm, not the fashion); they were the two main sets of customers, and they rubbed along well together – this was my grandmother's doing, really – although the farmers, very much alpha males, liked to fleece the townspeople at the Monday-night games of solo or brag. 'Don't play with them, boy, they'll have your bloody arms off,' was the warning from a sage old landowner to a sleek, suited man, who mused intelligently over each card – 'I'll keep that for future reference' – as his opponents moved in to fill their poachers' pockets.

The townspeople were frequently called to the telephone in the sitting room. Sometimes I was the person who had to go and find them. I once asked a man to go to the phone, thinking that he must be Mr X because he had his hand discreetly pushed up the jacket of the woman I knew to be Mrs X. This time the smiles were half-sly, half-embarrassed, but they did not falter.

Innately normal in their conversation and tastes, nonetheless these people inhabited a world of soap opera hysteria. It was as though they sought out melodrama – made it happen – as a constant act of rebellion against their *Daily Mail* and Marks & Spencer (St Michael) lives. Usually this took the tried and trusted form of adultery, played out half-publicly despite the reverence for concealment – car keys were seen to be thrown into ashtrays – and sometimes with an added extra, such as sleeping with two members of the same family. Such behaviour was in the scheme of things.

Any damage done was absorbed into the next few drinks. However, there was one woman, thin as a child, whose life plays out in my memory like a series of Hogarthian tableaux. She was married to a well-to-do businessman, a womaniser but not with any especial intent. Although she drank gin like it was going out of fashion, she was immaculate and good-natured; nevertheless, it came to the point where the husband, for reasons much whispered about, had had enough. Their divorce felt like a great rupture in the natural, acceptably flawed order. This pair had looked so twinned, with their wide starched collars and their glasses glistening with clean iced liquid; without the protection of ritual, the façade of a marriage in which certain things are understood and accepted, what might be unleashed? Plenty, as it happened. The woman took up with a bisexual man (said to run a local brothel) and had a baby. A couple of years after their wedding, the groom's boyfriend set fire to the marital home. The conflagration was blamed on the couple's toddler son. By this time the woman was drinking white wine, which in terms of sheer quantities seemed somehow worse than gin, and her huge lemur eyes had become both sad and unnerving (sitting quietly on the settle, good-natured still, she nonetheless shimmered with the tragicomic unpredictability of the drunkard). She was dead at fifty: one of those people who cannot rest until absolute destruction has been achieved. Obviously she would have done better never to visit any pub at all. Given that this was not going to happen, my grandmother's pub was probably her best option, something like a refuge.

It was understandable, therefore, that the third set of

customers should provide most of the subject matter for the kitchen chats.

In between the sounds of sizzling oil and banging plates, sentences would float through the door to the sitting room.

'She was properly gorn last night, wasn't she?'

'Oh yes. She'd been at it all day. And she gets nasty, in drink.'

A pause.

'Fancy someone like that having a baby, eh, Vi.'

'Um.' My grandmother could be heard opening the back door. 'That'll only get gin out of those tits.'

'I'm not sure Colin didn't go orf with her mum, you know.'

'Oh well—' (comfortably) '—she's a *real* tart, the mum.'

Or:

'I tell you what, Vi, I don't know how Sandra puts up with old Geoff, drive you mad, wouldn't he.'

'Coo hell. Wants a stick of dynamite up him.'

Or:

'*You* got caught, didn't you, Vi?'

Sometimes I could sense that a pause was my grandmother's way of wielding her power. Eventually, in a deliberately vague voice, she would concede: 'How do you mean, Rene?'

'I saw you got caught. Old what's her name – old Frances! Showing you her photos, wasn't she? I saw you there with her, she'd got you holed up in a corner.'

'Um…'

Bang, sizzle, bang. By my side the little dogs sighed and dreamed.

'What was it, her bloody honeymoon photos?'

Sometimes, by some means, I would catch on to whatever they were talking about: in this case I recalled that one of the old townsmen, named Eric, red and jolly and not unlike a bald Mr Punch, had recently married a woman named Frances, rather posh, as some of the customers were, and, like her husband, old and jolly. This marriage amazed me, of course, although I knew that I was wrong to think that way ('It's not only for young 'uns, you know').

What I also recalled, which I intuited would be relevant to this conversation, was an exchange some months earlier in which my grandmother had suggested, in her desultory way, that Eric was 'after' Irene. 'I reckon he's got his eye on you.' Irene had exploded quietly: 'Oh no, Vi, I couldn't fancy him. Ooh no, his old mouth and all.' 'Um... no, I know. Course, some women don't worry do they, they're not fussy...' She trailed off, as usual when contemplating the mystery of human nature. Then, voice in neutral: 'He's got a few bob.'

Now Irene was soliloquising: 'Well, old Frances didn't care about what he looked like, did she? Course he's got plenty, I remember you saying, got a nice house hasn't he, had a bit built on, didn't he, billiard room I reckon he said, bloody ridiculous but there you are, yes. I suppose she knew what she was doing...' The note of rage that always plucked at her remarks was well and truly dominant. 'Where'd they go, then, Madeira, wasn't it? Shouldn't have thought there was much to photograph there, a bit of sea, well we know what sea looks like...'

There was a brief pause, then my grandmother said decisively: 'I never said they were honeymoon photos, Rene. They *weren't* honeymoon photos.'

'Eh?'

There was the sound of a cup clinking in its saucer, marking a deliberate shift in the atmosphere. In a suddenly confiding tone my grandmother said: 'Tell you what though, they must be a right old pair, those two. I suppose that's how they got together, they're both sexy. Well, course, it's never the ones you think.'

'Eh? How do you mean?' Irene's voice was hoarse with intensity.

'She was only bloody showing me... you know, what she'd taken of him! Standing in the kitchen, he was. The kitchen! Hope there weren't any knives about... I'm sure I don't know why she wanted me to see. Showing orf, I suppose.'

'*Showing off?*'

'Well, you know, that they were still at it, type thing.'

A monumental clattering of the grill pan served to express Irene's ineffable emotions. 'Well, I'm sorry, Vi, but I've never heard the like. I mean, if they were young and, you know, nice – though why you'd want to do that, whatever for... But what a bloody liberty! Showing them to you!'

'Um.'

'I mean, whatever did you... No, that's what I can't get over, why she thinks you'd want to see him with nothing on... Him! I should have told her where she could stuff it...' The conversation had moved way beyond an appreciation of double entendres. 'Christ, you could chuck 'em out, nearly, for that...'

'Now don't be daft, Rene. They're good customers.'

'Good and bloody dirty.'

'No harm in it, is there? If that's what they want to do...'

A warning note had entered my grandmother's voice; again this was an obscure exertion of power. Then, after another short silence, she relented.

'Mind you. It wasn't much, his old thing.'

After a scuffling outburst of laughter the voices were definitively lowered, as if walls truly did have ears, and rose again only for a polite, innocuous remark that seemed to negate the previous conversation.

'Cup of rubbish, Rene?'

Rubbish was what my grandmother called Nescafé. Mostly the women drank gunpowder-strength coffee made in a huge percolator, but the palaver of filters was sometimes too much for them.

'Go on then, Vi.'

Oddly enough, my grandmother was herself something of a nudist. Some years later, at my parents' house, she wandered into the kitchen wearing only her anklet on her way to find a bath towel. Drinking tea at the table was a man who had come to do some building work. As a member of one of the farming families, he knew my grandmother very well from the pub, and he was a gentleman. 'Morning Violet,' he said, before returning to his *Racing Post*.

This nudism was, of course, nothing to do with sex. She was uninhibited, but she was never lewd. The private photoshoots of the old newlyweds – those sort of kicks, giggly and secretive but also seeking an audience – were not her style. I once asked her if she had enjoyed a particular night at the theatre, a revue show starring Mickey Rooney (she loved Hollywood), and she gave one of her slow, smiling, sorrowing shrugs. 'Um... Everything's *here*, you know' (pointing to her trouser zip). Max Miller, though... she had a passion for him. She had one of his concerts on an LP, a gift from her bank manager. Max Miller did innuendo like nobody else ('Cockfosters, lady? Go on, make something of that...') but with a quality that was utterly sane and healthy, as if shot through with the ozone of his native Brighton; like my grandmother he was louche but not prurient. Like her he celebrated and embraced human frailty with a warm cackle and a raised glass. The English used to be that way, robust and rich of blood; now, not so much.

My grandmother, who at the old pub had lent her black velvet evening dresses to the local homosexual couple, minded nothing about sex as long as people didn't make a display of themselves. Unnecessary, she thought, in a pub. Canoodling couples she hated. 'Oh, we've all done that,' she would say, actually shoving her way between them. 'We've all had abortions!' She was given to remarks of that airily unexplained kind. Respecting her code as I did, I would never have asked what she meant by them.

For although I am nostalgic for her – something she would have liked but not really understood – I have no desire to research her. I simply present her, as she presented herself to me, as I remember her at the pub.

In the school holidays, while waiting for my mother (who visited the pub regularly but as family; she was not a pub person), I went on errands to 'the shop', a tiny general store at the end of the village road, where the woodland cast its heavy shadows. The woman who ran it was eccentric. She kept the place locked until a customer was pressing their face against the window. My grandmother's lists – in her dreadful handwriting, the product of her non-schooling – were magnificent and to me slightly frightening: *3 or 4 BIG lemons. Vim. Pickle. Big Jar Gerkins.* Pears SOFT. *Anything nice.* I would sometimes see Irene examining my offerings with narrow eyes, testing a pear for ripeness, finding it inadequate.

On school days my grandmother would drive me in the MG, or sometimes Victor would do so. In so far as she had one, he was her man.

Their long affair had begun during the war, when she had returned to her favoured status of *dauphine* – queen in all but name – at the old pub. There Victor encountered her, gleaming behind the bar: her hair, like her floor-length dresses, raven-black. Victor had a wife, to whom he quite literally never spoke, and as soon as he was free he offered marriage to my grandmother, also newly divorced. She refused ('never again'). This was the irony: for all her repetition of 'you've got to have a man', her own life was independent. She and Victor remained together, however, despite numerous other suitors including a headmaster, a well-known boxer, a handsome farmer from a neighbouring village who later hanged himself, the captain of a ship on which she took a cruise, and an impresario named Nat Tennens, who owned the Kilburn Empire. He was very rich. She could have given up work and shopped at Harrods every day. 'I took him to the Licensed Victuallers' ball. Oh, he was mad after me... I told him I was married.' It was true, in a way: she was married to the pub.

Experience had honed my grandmother's natural gift for cutting to the heart of character and situation. 'Well, she's like a tart, isn't she,' or, 'He doesn't know what time of day it is,' or, 'Course, she's got all the money,' or, 'Oh yes, Uncle Arthur, he carried on with his niece, but he was lovely,' or – a favoured diagnosis, used of anybody who talked too much or laughed too loudly: 'Nerves.' She did the same for people in books and films. 'That's told you, mate,' I once overheard her say to the television screen, as she neared the end of a solitary viewing of *Onegin*, and watched Tatiana show the door to the now supplicant Eugene. These judgments left no room for ambivalence, but they always hit the mark. So, had she been discussing herself in the kitchen, with the same considered dispassion that she showed towards everybody else, she would undoubtedly have said: 'Well, she never really wanted anyone, did she.'

At the time I am describing, Victor's role in my grandmother's life was indeterminate. He was affable, and spry as a show dog, even as he ate the sweating triangles of the bacon sandwich served to him in the morning. For some reason I thought him slightly silly. He was displaced, no doubt, hanging around this little village. He lived nearby, was well-to-do, having inherited some business or other that he later sold, but like my grandmother he was London-born and carried an air of the city; also of what my father called 'razzmatazz'. He had been a jazz guitarist and had played with Louis Armstrong – 'Lewis' – on a tour of England. He could wander down Denmark Street and be glad-handed by fellow musicians; could float backstage and be welcomed by bandleaders like Bert Ambrose. He knew people such as Harry Lewis, who had played in the Ambrose orchestra and married Vera Lynn. This was the kind of thing that my grandmother liked about Victor, and that he liked to talk about, although he maintained a certain elegant reticence. I had a place at ballet school, which meant that he would tell me about all about his brother, who had been a champion dancer alongside the young Lew Grade ('you know, the telly feller'), and about the people he and my grandmother had 'seen': Hutch, Beatrice Lillie, Pearl Bailey, Danny Kaye (such a sell-out sensation that they had watched him standing at the back of the theatre, next to Harry and Vera). These names meant nothing to me, although I was keen on hearing about Fonteyn and Nureyev. Nevertheless, Victor's papery skin and 'Palladium suits' (my father again) were a bit too much for me. At this point I could only deal with adultness when I was observing it from a protected position.

Victor spent pub mornings at a dapper loose end: rustling the paper, smoking with urbane dedication, walking a hundred yards up the road with Tom (not Ted) twinkling beside him on a diamanté-spangled lead. Meanwhile at around ten my grandmother – sallow-faced, silk scarf over her curlers – would emerge into the bar. With the air of concentration that made one slightly wary, she prepared for opening while I watched from my place on one of the settles. She was framed like a painting by the shelf of glasses overhead and the walls to either side, and her movements were dashing, efficient, superbly womanly. She would take down the bottles that hung behind the bar, unscrew the optics and top up the contents through a funnel – Gordon's, Bells, Teacher's, Courvoisier, Beefeater (not that anyone ever drank Beefeater) – as a thin, spirituous smell rose into the air like a spell. Then she would cut up slices of lemon, spear cherries, tip bags of sour coppers into the huge till. Her impatient hand rubbed a pad of Duraglit over the special tankards and wiped an old dishcloth around the ashtrays, which remained damp throughout the mornings. The bar was still grey at this point, its spark unlit.

When she had applied her red lipstick, the only point of colour in the bar, she pulled back the heavy bolts on the pub doors. At the very moment of opening, the local butcher would enter in his apron.

Civilly, with an air of mild surprise at his own request, he would ask for a whisky. 'Large one, Vi, while you're there.'

Then he would have another double, meanwhile conversing about the weather or some such topic.

Then he would have another. Then – it was by now about 11 a.m. – he would produce an empty half-bottle from his apron pocket, and pleasantly ask my grandmother to fill it with Teacher's. This she did, as between them the atmosphere remained that of a garden tea party. Finally the butcher would walk, with a minimally lurching gait, out of the pub, and up towards the road.

Once, after this performance, Irene had ventured the comment: 'Drunken old bugger.' It had not gone down well with my grandmother. The butcher, in her view, adhered to the code of the pub: he was an entirely gentlemanly alcoholic, and criticism was therefore entirely out of place.

Morning trade... the crack of the door-latches was always a sound of promise, but this was an extraordinary testament to the optimism generated by pubs. So often it was unfulfilled. The stage had been perfectly prepared, but the show was reluctant to take wing. The very light was uncertain of its role: the pub demanded that it dimple and glow, but pragmatic day refused to give way: the soft electric gleam behind the counter had not yet spread through the bars. They were rooms, rather than rich little treasure boxes. The air was parched. The darkness held no mystery; the wedges of sun that sliced through it showed up worn patches of carpet, ash stains, wrinkles, the creep of steel-grey at the hair roots, all the imperfections and weaknesses that the pub – in its infinite knowing humanity – was there to forgive. The thing had not yet *come together*. Irene, perched on a stool behind the bar like a tough old parrot, smoked her St Moritz and rustled viciously at the *Daily Express* as time moved at a stately *andante* pace: in accordance with pub tradition the clock above the fireplace was kept about eight minutes fast, so the joy of seeing its hands move was tempered by the knowledge that they told a permanent lie. Victor, his black coffee thick with undissolved sugar crystals, sat on a companion stool at the saloon bar counter, smiling gamely at nothing, blowing smoke into the emptiness. My grandmother, in her role of impresario, would march in and out from backstage, carrying cheese and gherkins with the chihuahuas pattering at her heels. The show looked like a failure, killed at birth in fact, but she was undaunted. She would assess the scene with a cool eye, as if faintly disgusted by the failure of her public to do its bit, before demanding that the music (muzac really, a bold lapse of taste) be turned up and illusions created. In the sitting room I would watch from the window, with its sumptuously sagging velvet curtains and half-covering of soft peach chiffon. And slowly, one by one, the morning regulars would come up the road, looking towards the pub as if it were their sole destiny, yet at the same time affecting a kind of nonchalance, as if they had just happened to be passing and thought, why not?

Poignant, this was. I knew it even then, although I did not know why. There were three morning customers in particular who occupied the settle in the public bar, in alliance and yet in solitude. A sad little woman with scanty permed hair who drank Double Diamond. To her left, a man with a pipe, defiant in his lack of charm. To her right, a man who communed with his pint and his Embassy as if they alone could comprehend his memories of years as a POW. The little woman smiled sweetly and humbly at everybody who passed, including the chihuahuas. She could wring five minutes' worth of activity from asking if somebody was 'all right' (shifting in her seat and repositioning her Double Diamond before saying it; getting her eye in properly with the person before saying it; actually saying it – almost inaudibly, as it happened, but with the urgent mouth movements of a novice practitioner of sign language; saying it again, if there was the slightest doubt that she had been received the first time; smiling with vehement satisfaction at the reply of 'Yes, fine'; waiting with terrible eagerness for the retaliatory 'Are *you* all right?' which occasionally failed to come; deploying ever more urgent sign language for the reply of 'Oh, *I'm* all right!'; sighing and settling back in her seat; casting half-embarrassed smiles around the bar at a mission successfully accomplished; exchanging a deprecatory glance with the pipe-smoker, who would be staring at her as if she had gone temporarily mad; taking a long sip of Double Diamond in the self-conscious manner of one who had just correctly intercepted a starter question on *University Challenge*; winding down with a quietly agitated half-minute of glass adjustment, beer mat study and fidgeting her soft-soled shoes). She bought her round, taking her money from a purse full of Green Shield stamps, although in a gesture of grudging gallantry the pipe-smoker would go to the bar on her behalf. When it was his turn to pay he would say to her: 'You having another one, then? You'll be on the floor with them dogs,' or some such thing, at which she would laugh in a bruised, brave, 'hark at him' way with anybody who caught her eye. When the ex-POW went to the bar he would command the attention of Irene, or whoever it might be, with a sharply mumbled: '*Achtung!*' Back in his seat he might say: 'What's today? ... Today's *Freitag*.' Other than that he barely spoke.

What were these three people doing there? Drinking, one might say: these were the days before alcohol could be bought at every pit-stop. Drinking, of course. But drink and pubs are not the same thing. Co-dependent, but different. The butcher's desire for alcohol was clothed in a ritual courtesy, a public dimension imposed by the public house. The pub was doing something more for the threesome on the settle than selling them beer; it was assuaging something more complicated than mere loneliness.

Not that it brought pleasure, exactly. The proper pub is about far more than having a good time. It accommodates the miserable, the misfits, those who are in their seats at curtain up, having nothing in their lives to make them late: from the moment of waking, they are waiting for the moment of opening. By the fireplace in the public bar was a small table with its own stool. This was the domain of another morning regular, an old farmer with a fearsome face beneath his tweed cap, who would bang on the table with his stick when he wanted a drink. He was the only person who didn't approach the counter. He hated everybody – although he eased off a little at the sight of my grandmother – and apparently hated being in the pub. 'How much?' was his response to every request for payment. 'Can't drink that, woman, it's flat as a bloody pancake/got too much bloody head on it,' was the usual reaction to his pint.

Yet his dogged appearance every day was courageous. In he staggered, on brittle legs, roaring and spitting and, in his way, doing his bit. 'Old sod,' my grandmother would say, when Irene reported the latest complaint about the beer, but this was token. In her early years at the pub, she and the farmer had shared a telephone line. They went way back, to the time when the pub had been patronised only by country people, and she took him for all in all. The same thing with the threesome on the settle. 'Poor old sods.' She had a brisk compassion for the needy, never dirtied by the urge to patronise. So too did the livelier people who began to gladden the look of the place around midday: the exquisite mistress with the high grey chignon, giving out smiles like a film star meeting the England football team; her blazered paramour, offering drinks all round in a pantomime of manly nods and winks. With this smooth invasion, the tick-tocking strain of the morning began to ease. Irene would hop from her stool and pour Victor a Guinness, which he sipped with his habitual air of experienced discrimination. From the sitting room I would hear the discreet hum, punctuated by little bursts of adult laughter, signifying that the show was on the road. Now came the comfortable crunch of wheels on the car park tarmac, the generous swoop of Rovers and Jaguars. Now the morning regulars, arranged around the edges of the bar, became so many staring gargoyles. They had played their part, nevertheless: more than anybody, they proved the value of the pub, and by turning up when it would have been easier to stay cloistered at home in front of *Crown Court*, they earned its venial sanctuary.

'No place like home when you've got nowhere else to go,' my great-grandfather used to say. He had understood very well the not-quite-home essence of the pub. The morning regulars did not leave the house tricked out with paint or charm; unlike most of the customers, they had no public self to offer up for consumption. Yet they were still, by the mere fact of being out, not quite their private selves. Something was on display, however little that was. It is brave, really, to want to enter a public arena without any of the conventional armour. The sad-eyed woman who drank Double Diamond displayed all the quotidian valour of my grandmother, with none of the scented swagger to help her along. In a way that she would not have bothered or wanted to explain, my grandmother recognised this, and respected the woman accordingly.

At 2.30 p.m. the pub closed, and even in summer the air hung dully. In the little sitting room, where velvet now muffled the windows, Irene and my grandmother ate their proper lunches – the big meal of the day – while the chihuahuas crouched hopefully at their feet ('Christ, Vi, don't give Ted anything, his belly'll burst,' Irene would remark). Then the women retreated into immobility, corpse-like, their cream-covered faces surrounded by a halo of curlers, their only movements the languid stretch of hands towards cups of tea. They dozed as some unspeakable television programme, such as *Love Boat*, murmured in the background and flickered greenish-indigo in the dusk.

Saturdays were different: livelier. Victor was in attendance, seated at the gatefold table, his cufflinks catching the light as he manhandled the *Sporting Life*. He had a Ladbrokes telephone account that they all used for their bets. This was natural to them, a natural component of pub life. So too were days at the races. My grandmother had gone to the Derby before the war; people went en masse from the old pub, as did so many when the race was run on a Wednesday and briefly stopped the nation in a collective, pub-like way. From the sixties onwards she favoured a day out at Royal Ascot, which in those days was purposeful, smart and wonderfully unlike the fancy dress party cum al fresco nightclub that it now resembles. Sometimes she went with my parents, sometimes in a minibus with a driver. One year, a minibus year around the time that I am describing, she and a few friends – Irene and Victor included – stopped off for a couple of drinks on the way back from the racecourse. There was a particular pub, somewhere near Slough, that she remembered with her characteristic astringent affection; in fact she had visited it with one of her suitors, the well-known boxer whose bruised eyes had regarded her with such adoration.

Apparently the place retained its charm. Yet it was transfigured by the unnatural conviviality that arises when a pub is filled with customers who do not know each other but have all attended the same event. People at the bar jabbered hysterically about 20/1 wins, short-head losses, Lester Piggott, the Queen. Friendships were made, cards exchanged, rendezvous agreed and assuredly not kept. Meanwhile my grandmother's party – a touch weary but still keeping its end up – had taken possession of a large table, which they bountifully shared with what at first seemed to be a smiling band of jolly, lairy, harmless cockneys, and were gradually revealed to be a smiling collection of serious London gangsters. Their true calling emerged, like sun with the dispersal of mist, as the supporting cast of innocent racegoers faded out of the pub and left it denuded, almost silent, with nothing to camouflage the unmistakable demeanour of these men. By then my grandmother's party quite fancied leaving as well. However, the gangsters were the kind who didn't let people do that. The pub grew quieter and quieter, the talk at the table more effortful and desultory, but the night, like Dorian Gray, remained horribly young. '*Don't* be daft, you don't want to go yet… what're you *having?* Come on, put that away… don't be *daft*… your money ain't no good in here…' Familiar pub talk – with a twist. From my grandmother's telling of the story, what had bothered her most was this refusal to let her party buy a round. The breach of etiquette, the indebtedness, seemed especially heinous in such company. Eventually, after she had been winking crossly at him for about two hours, Victor managed to buy some champagne – 'Go on then, feller, if you must' – and once this was poured out, the landlord, thinking to hasten the evening to its longed-for conclusion, collected a long broom and began to sweep cautiously around the bar. It might have worked, but it didn't. One of the gangsters put down his champagne (into which he had carefully mixed a very great deal of brandy), rose from his stool and walked over to the landlord. With his cigarette between his teeth he took hold of the broom, snapped it calmly in two and hurled both pieces through a closed window. 'That's fucking woman's work,' he said to the landlord, as one imparting a piece of vitally important advice.

This incident, and the accompanying shatter of glass around the table, allowed my grandmother's party to break the magnetic spell holding them to their seats at speed to the car park. I very much doubt that she was frightened. In all the time that I knew her she was never frightened of anything, and anyway she would have known that these men adhered to the gangster code – a brutish, sentimental variation on the pub code – that required them to respect ladies, and indeed old sorts like Victor.

What perturbed her (because she lost her sense of humour when recalling the evening) was something harder to define, a kind of disrespect for this particular pub, which had been part of her legend, and with that for the whole concept of the 'nice' pub, the 'good house', which she herself represented. She probably also felt that the situation had been her fault, which it would have been. I could just imagine her sitting expansively at the table, dominating and bestowing herself, telling stories in her well-phrased, solipsistic way, conjuring the Slough pub in the old days, when it was run by a family ('beautiful people') and loved by the well-known boxer ('Oh yes, we courted for a while, well I was a good looker then, you know'; 'You still are my darling'; etc). The tough London men would have smiled at her in a rapt, glint-toothed manner, and all in all she would have greatly enjoyed holding them in her thrall. Few people liked an audience more than she. In fact she had been 'showing orf', as she called it, and in the end she had got what the gangsters would have called 'her uppingtons'.

I never actually heard Irene say, 'Well it was you who got in with them, wasn't it, Vi,' but she might as well have done, because she would so obviously have been thinking it.

Of course my grandmother, who covered life with strong brushstrokes, knew all about criminals. There were several in her pub, most of whom she treated with an impeccable guarded friendliness. One man went to jail, for reasons much whispered about in the kitchen (receiving, is my adult interpretation), and a year later returned to the pub with the same smile beneath fearful eyes. My grandmother was vaguely contemptuous of the legal system that had locked him up. 'Poor old sod, he was just the one that got caught.' This remark may have been obscurely aimed at Irene and the spiv husband – almost certainly Irene would have taken it that way – but it was also true that other pub customers did similar, or worse. When I look back I can pick out the apprehension in certain faces, the townsmen in supple leather whose largesse depended upon dodges and effrontery. In the kitchen there were subdued whisperings that I didn't begin to understand – 'He only rents that Jag, you know'; or 'He put it all through the casino, didn't he'; or 'He did it in her name, I reckon' – although as so often I caught something of what was meant, that such-and-such a person carried a weight of wary guilt beneath his bonhomie. It was the kind of behaviour that modern puritanism vilifies. The pub forgave it.

It was human nature, after all, lax and imperfect and susceptible. My grandmother accepted it as such: *c'était son métier*. What she could not accept was conduct that transgressed against her code, such as brooms through windows. And nothing of that kind ever occurred in her establishment. A pub finds its level. She was vulnerable, in a way that a landlord would simply not have been – when all was said and done she was a small, middle-aged woman, with guard dogs the size of Toby jugs – but the threat of 'trouble' walking in remained existential. In some ineffable way my grandmother set standards as palpable as the strong brick walls of the bar. They did not preclude bad behaviour, but they frowned upon its display. That doesn't mean that it *wasn't* displayed, but there was a knowledge that it should not have been.

It can't have been easy for her, embodying that code. Despite her bright confidence, her tough and elastic sense of self, she was surely aware that the pub, her own home after all, was an arena that absolutely anybody might enter; the edifice she had created was a mighty one but it was also a construct, built on faith, in which her customers had chosen to believe. It was a theatrical performance, an illusion that anybody, at any moment, could walk onstage and destroy. And there was – I now recall – a brief period, when the pub was patronised by a bunch of men who arrived on motorbikes, all smiles and 'get one for the lady', but importing a wayward, uneasy atmosphere, a shard of carelessness and danger. Suddenly it seemed as if fragile little worlds, like that of the old threesome on the settle, could be shattered as easily as the painstakingly polished glasses above the counter. Which they could, in fact. Only a tacit respect for something impossible to define kept it all intact. The men did not stick around, so my grandmother must have won the battle of wills. She could not throw them out, but she could freeze them out. Not easy, as I say: this was her own house, but it was a public house, and balancing those two concepts – public versus house – was at the heart of her landlady's gift.

The threat of the motorbike men was very simple: there were too many of them. In ones or twos they would have been containable. It was a question of balance, as so often with pubs. Although my grandmother liked most of her customers (kitchen remarks notwithstanding), a few of them stood on the cusp of unacceptability, but as individuals they could be absorbed – just. She knew that her private judgments had to be weighed against the fact that the pub did not judge. And so – for instance – she smiled her welcome at a man whose family she had known for years, who one day killed his wife, and who returned to the pub after a sentence not much longer than that of the man who dealt in stolen goods (he had pleaded provocation). Quite soon he was flourishing a companion, an attractive woman whom he had met through a dating agency. He was liberated in every sense, wildly cheerful, his ebullience occasionally streaked with something jagged, like lightning in a sky. He troubled my grandmother. Morals were not her business, but they were when they equated to inappropriate pub conduct. Surely a wife-killer should not behave as this man did, drinking champagne like tap water, laughing uproariously then lapsing into sad, head-shaking memories of 'when my wife died'? In the kitchen she would mutter over his bizarre *chutzpah* and worry away at the mentality of the woman who had assumed the role of his new companion and who, it was gradually established, knew his past ('Um . . .

kinky, I suppose'). She feared that customers would be put off by him, but of course everybody was deeply interested. Some years later – again at Ascot – my parents and I were transfixed by the sight of the wife-killer in high good humour, entertaining his lady friend in the Royal Enclosure. He was evicted quite quickly, not on account of being a murderer, but because he was wearing a borrowed badge.

Another man, fairly steeped in Aramis, was said to be an arms dealer. I only knew this much later. The kitchen whispers about him were very quiet. There was none of the appalled levity with which they discussed a pretty girl, ex-wife of one of the regulars, who was rumoured to work as a prostitute in a Mayfair hotel; or indeed the wife-killer, who was at least a known criminal quantity, and had served his time. An arms dealer was altogether different, casting a shadow too deep for accommodation, like that of a noose against a prison wall. Again, my grandmother was not comfortable. I can recall a preoccupied stillness when the man put his arm round her. But he rubbed her shoulder fondly and paid for his drinks – lots of them – so what was she to do? He had a saturnine face, crunched into watchful smiles, and a big body that women seemed to like. A rather flash, lean girlfriend would occasionally zoom up in her TR7 and stake her claim. More usually the man was surrounded by a harem of housewives, flirting with him rather anxiously; later I learned that a couple of babies, raised as legitimate, were in fact his; perhaps the husbands didn't dare to say anything. Looking back, I think they were wise. I can see him now, a man whose appearance was just this side of respectable: huge, swarthy head bent to avoid the beams, eyes dark and hollow, hands like implements around a long glass of Bacardi and a female breast. I can feel the danger of him. One of his associates, an insignificant type occasionally seen in the pub, took the rap and went to jail on his account, then emerged to buy a nearby manor house the size of a small stately home. The man himself died quite young.

Sundays at the pub were not days of rest – they did not exist, except when my grandmother escaped to the south of France – but they were her retreat from people of that kind. She asserted her own values, secular and sacred. When afternoon closing time came ('P.O.!' she would say gaily from the window, meaning piss off, as the customers lurched across the car park), there was no post-lunch submergence into the sitting room. Instead my grandmother took over her saloon bar, covered a couple of the wooden tables with a thick cloth and set up a card school. I can't have spent so many Sundays at the pub, but for some reason this is one of my strongest memories. Crack, crack, went the door latch, a sound of joyful conspiracy at this hour, and into the plush silence came women of my grandmother's rich vintage: heads tilted, eyes bird-bright, carrying their years not as burdens, but like suitcases on a still fascinating journey. One, pungent with charm and self-mockery, had learned to fly a plane and joined the ATA during the war. The others were sisters, May and Margot, both pub women. Margot had been walking back to her establishment after an air raid, and from the top of the road had watched a last stray bomb – an afterthought, as it were – fall straight onto the pub, killing her husband and mother. But she was jolly now, full of the pub's quotidian valour. 'Hallo, Vi, darling!' she exclaimed as she waddled in, arms outstretched, her pink scalp visible beneath the Victorian-doll waves of her hair. 'Oh your hair's beautiful, Marg.' Margot and her sister had dry carmine lips and puffed, floury cheeks. They wore close-fitting dresses in heavy textured stuff, the kind of material no longer seen, and court shoes gamely shoehorned onto plump feet. The ATA lady wore rakish trouser suits. 'Don't you look lovely, darling!' 'Don't *you*.' From their gold-clasped handbags they proffered pound notes for the kitty, which my grandmother would change at the till.

In the soft maroon light the women played hand after hand of solo. This was the jazzed-up form of bridge that they favoured, with an opaque terminology – *misère, misère ouvert* ('mizzair of air', as they pronounced it), *abondance*, royal abundance – which I prided myself on understanding. Victor was usually there, a solitary male presence, adding a courtly zest to proceedings. He would play a hand or two; people took it in turn to sit out, nursing whichever of the dogs was not asleep on my grandmother. The visitors were extremely kind to me, especially when I handed round tea and cake in the dark blue-and-gilt Royal Albert (no alcohol was taken). But this was an adult occasion, and from my stool just inside the fireplace I simply breathed it all in.

The traditions of solo were fiercely revered. There was, for instance, a special shuffle. Unorthodoxy was frowned upon – 'What ever did you go *misère* for, with that hand?' –

as was the least lapse in attention. 'What the bloody hell did you go and lead that spade for? You knew she didn't have any.' 'How did I know that?' 'Well I bloody knew, I suppose I was paying attention.' The worst sin was 'revoking': not following suit. 'You revoked!' Not that these women ever revoked (that was me, twenty years later). My grandmother used certain phrases when she played cards, sincerely but to droll comedic purpose. 'Coo, *hang*,' she would say, when she picked up a bad hand, and 'You can sod orf,' when she played a two, and 'Oo-er', when somebody played a trump. The game was deeply serious, but as a ritual. Post-mortems were conducted after each hand, sometimes with a degree of rancour instilled by Irene, but this meant little. What signified was a shared sensibility. Again there was nothing elegiac in the atmosphere; these people were too engaged with the present for that. They conjured memories in a spirit of self-affirmation, and buoyed themselves with a sense of lives fully lived: then and now, then as now.

'Do you remember that pub we used to go to in London? Jack Straw's, the Swiss, the York Minster?... That pub near Slough, where that lovely boxer went drinking, where we got tangled up with all those bloody villains?' (thus the rogue evening was nullified)... 'That pub round this way, old Frank's, you know, who was after Vi?' 'Oh Frank, oh. He was a lovely feller. Oh tsk, I should love to see him again'... 'You'll have to dig him up if you want to see him, Vi... You missed your chance there...'

Laughter, warm rippling cascades of it, like the generous trickle of spirits into a glass. Frank was under the ground, and they were sorry about that, but they were still above it, in all their vigour: the landladies and their friends, enjoying a hand of solo and a bit of good company, celebrating the human urge towards pleasure. This was the pub code, all right. From my place inside the stone fire I entertained thoughts that were treacherous, observing the split seam beneath Margot's armpit that crept further open with every mouthful of cake, the weary creases in Victor's hitherto impeccable suit, the clownish black line of the ATA lady's artificial eyebrows; and I wondered how they kept going with their rhythmic, throaty jokes when part of them (I could see it) longed for the enveloping dressing gown and the television screen. I was tired myself. I was finding it hard to hide the fact. But these people did, and how I admired them! Even in this out-of-hours gathering the women were putting on a show: for themselves, for the man with his head inclined attentively towards them, for each other. They all knew that life dropped bombs, but what went on in their dark hours they kept to themselves, because what made life bearable was the show, the façade; not the same thing as shallowness.

The women would have a drink after opening. Naturally. The plate of cheese would come out of the larder with certain Sunday embellishments, perhaps olives from Harrods, which the ATA lady would examine as if with a wink. Like my grandmother, she could make every moment a priceless little nugget of fun. 'Shall we drown a couple of those in a gin and French, Vi?' Magic words. The modishness of gin today would have amused my grandmother: she knew that it was more important than that. Its thick translucence was the taste of life to her – melancholy, buoyancy – and the very idea of gin and French represented all about life that she loved: it was Wheeler's and Sheekey's and pools of city light; it was the moment in a day when the sky began to turn navy and time stood upon a brink; it was the rich red smear on a brittle glass, a dark piano played in a dusky room, Gershwin and Bix Beiderbecke and Dinah Washington. It was pleasure – an acute liver-deep sharpness, followed by a spread into warmth – for which a price was worth paying; indeed the price, the aftermath, was part of the pleasure.

My grandmother made a martini in her own way, so strong that it tasted only of strength. It was, she averred – again in her own way, which admitted of no dissent – the most beautiful drink known to man. 'Hope I die with one in my hand.' Both she and the ATA lady took their first sip with their eyes closed, in reverence.

The weekday transition into evening opening was entirely different, and from my position on the sofa I saw the effort with which it was made. It was the only time that I was aware of my grandmother's mortality, when she trudged up the stairs with her back bent and a cup of tea rattling on its saucer in her hand. The doll's house staircase lay behind a wooden door in the sitting room. The landing – a white stone tunnel, with a slanted ceiling and floorboards that seemed to bend beneath one's feet – led to two bedrooms and an enormous bathroom; very little of this had existed when my grandmother took over the pub. The space that the bathroom now occupied had been a giant hole above the sitting room, where the ceiling had reached up to the roof. That was how basic the pub had been when she first went there, and how tough she had been not to be daunted by this alien rural place, but instead to fill it with her robust urban soul. The bathroom, for instance… what a bathroom she made for herself, on top of the ancient black beams! Like her it was luxurious, casually grand and unworried by bourgeois considerations: thickly carpeted and marbled, heady and humid from the airing cupboard, sweet with the smell of sodden soap and Gordon Moore toothpaste (magenta in colour, bought from Harrods). Tiny colourless spiders lived in every cracked corner, and danced in the bath every morning.

Depending on her mood, I might sit on my grandmother's satin bedspread – a deep rose colour, with pale, worn seams – and watch her making-up at her dressing table. Wonderful she looked, a businesslike enchantress in the relaxing gloom, surrounded by the paraphernalia of female transformation: tarnished silver brushes, heavy gold bracelets that she would push up on to arms as shiny as snakeskin. I frankly deified her at those times. She was nearly sixty but she was still bold, still worth looking at. Something of the essence of glamour had settled itself inside her. She rubbed and jabbed at her supple olive face while a Player's leaked tar into an ashtray. Everything about my grandmother was made of a richer material than those of today – all that she wore, all that surrounded her was silken or satiny or iridescent or prismatic, substantial and dense and pierced with her life-force – she belonged to a world before the matte, the neutral, the greige and the minimalist. She was Harrods in the days when one walked in sumptuous silence on green patterned carpet, Selfridges in the days when one lunched in the stately high-ceilinged Orchard restaurant; she was life in the days when it was lived; the world to which she belonged was already passing, but with what admirable assurance she put the new one in its place!

Downstairs Irene, whose red waves had at last sprung angrily free of their curlers, would be readying the pub for opening. Although the women were primed for this second performance, they were also oddly resistant; obliged though they were to unlatch the doors, they almost always exerted the power not to do so, reclaiming a few precious autonomous minutes during which they behaved in a quite extraordinary manner, like truanting schoolgirls. It was an evening thing, to do with the lights. By six these should have been switched on. But the pub remained defiantly dark, disguising itself (inn sign notwithstanding) as a shadowy old house by the side of the road. Both women would stand at a window – Irene in the sitting room, my grandmother in her bedroom – and watch who was approaching the pub. As in the morning, the first customer usually came on foot, their arrival timed precisely for six. If it was the wrong person, the sort of person who made punctuality into something irritating and a bit pitiable, the lights would not go on. The women would hiss up and down the stairs at each other – 'It's old Glyn!'; 'Don't open up, Rene. Let him P.O.!' – and Irene would shield herself behind the sitting-room curtains. 'Has he gorn, Rene?' 'Hang on – he's hanging about… Right, he's gone.'

'Greedy old sod, I'm not opening up for him.'

How the customers put up with this, I have no idea, but they sort of loved it. Their power came from the fact that they knew exactly what was happening, and could see the dark female shapes peering and hiding at the windows. Again the whole performance was part of my grandmother's landlady legend. Ten minutes later old Glyn, or old Pete, or old Clifford would be back, making his way along the road in a haze of hope, already mentally tasting his first sip of pint, all the more sublime for its deferral.

Then the evening would begin. Slowly, at the start. I would hear the arrhythmic clicks of the door latches and the forced, halting conversation ('All right?' 'Not too bad'; or, when the customer was of the waggish variety: 'Not three bad'). This was the hour of the pub nuisance, such as the man who, when asked how he was – not that anybody wanted details – would eye the questioner sincerely and explain, with an air of jocund pedantry, that his day had been marred by a 'traumatic experience', which he would then describe.

The early evening might also attract a brighter breed, however: the man (it was always a man) who was on his way home from work, and who sought a calm, civilised, pint-enhanced breathing space. He could have had this drink at home, but the whole point was to have it at a pub. My father did this regularly. He and his suited kind brought in a stimulating air of elsewhere, of a day spent in taxing but satisfying business, of relaxation earned. As I now know, there is no taste like that of the first drink after a proper day's work, the absolute sensuality with which alcohol pierces sobriety. The second drink is different altogether: a delightful continuation, imparting a sense of increase, of thickening and spreading; the third is like the second, except more so; then things start to change. Usually (not always) one drink was enough for my father. He went home, his state pleasantly altered. It was something that only pubs can do.

By that time, the chief barmaid, Marian, would have arrived. She was a splendid Valkyrie dressed by Miss Selfridge, a single mother who lived with her baby in a caravan and whom I rather worshipped. My grandmother thought the world of her. 'Smashing girl.' Marian would take up her stance behind the counter, Benson & Hedges between two long fingers, bending this way and that to pull a pint or push a glass against an optic. She stood framed, dispenser of favours and recipient of admiration: a 'proper' barmaid, in my grandmother's estimation, who could angle a glass beneath the pump and achieve the perfect three-quarter inch of clean white head. The remarks that were made to her – 'Two large ones, girl. Nothing personal' – would today lead to a lawsuit, but in those days were delivered almost in a spirit of duty, as part of the role in which men were then cast. Marian fenced with them all amiably, wryly, her eyes withdrawn behind their yashmak of cigarette smoke. One of her suitors was the man who went to jail for the arms dealer. He sat at the bar, full of his secrets, with apparently nothing on his mind beyond the conquest of Marian. The intensity of his gaze upon her was par for the course; nevertheless, my grandmother was on the alert to any customer who crossed the indefinable, yet to her perfectly clear, line between male silliness and male liberty-taking. 'Would you like it if some feller spoke to your old woman like that?' she once snapped. The man in question subsided, just like the head on a pint. I never saw anybody summon the guts to talk back to my grandmother.

Having stood behind a bar from the age of fifteen, she knew the peculiar position in which the barmaid was placed, protected yet vulnerable, in command yet subservient: the very word *serve*, as in serving a customer, implied low status. Not that my grandmother had ever been so exposed. As landlady (before that as landlord's daughter) she and the pub were an indissoluble entity. From her high-priestess position behind the counter she would address any unfamiliar man as 'sir', flourishing the word like a posy – 'Evening, sir'; 'Cold old night, sir'; 'Now what can I get you, sir?' – but she said it with an easy, emphatic, stagey courtesy that made of deference something dominant: the man thus addressed was somehow turned into the supplicant.

By the time that I am describing, her appearances behind the bar had acquired the air of a star actress taking a brief cameo role. More usually it was Irene (her eyes occasionally narrowing in the direction of my grandmother's stool) who lifted the hatch and 'went round', although supplementary to Marian was a second girl, Aileen, who worked three nights a week. She was full-figured and supremely efficient, apparently all set up to be a proper barmaid, but her dark eyes glowered at the customers beneath their plucked brows; one could imagine her face as the photofit of a suspected murderess. 'Go on girl, crack a smile,' the farmers would say. 'Look, she's got teeth, I knew they were in there.' Aileen featured quite regularly in the kitchen conversations, although not as often as she would later do. It was suspected at first that her ill temper derived from hunger – she had confessed that she was 'doing Slimfast', a regime of diet drinks – but she remained so substantial that it was decided, by my grandmother, that she was having the drinks as adjuncts to her usual meals. Aileen's dourness, it seemed, was her nature. 'She upset old Pete,' Irene would say. 'Turned nasty when he said his pint was flat. Shame, eh?' Despite herself, my grandmother would occasionally gulp down one of Irene's tactically placed acid drops. 'It's not so easy, getting barmaids! What am I supposed to do? How many do you think there are like Marian, how would I find another one like her?' 'Oh, yes, I know.' Irene always backpedalled, instantly emollient, in order to return with renewed momentum. 'Course, Marian has to do it, doesn't she, with the kid?'

On one unremarkable weekday evening, one of the regulars – a taciturn, unobtrusive, solitary man – left to drive home after closing; as the lights of the car fell across the window, a tremendous thud was heard. The remaining customers dashed to the door. Aileen was lying across the man's car bonnet, all fifteen stone of her, unhurt and shouting her head off. In a fit of passion she had hurled herself at his windscreen. Nobody knew the prequel to this event; nobody had known that the silent man was her errant lover: it was a rare and remarkable failure of pub acumen. Of course it had seemed that customer lust was directed solely at the comely Marian, with Aileen untroubled by such considerations. As for the man, smiling secretly into his pint while his fellow drinkers hollered and joked and boasted, he too had been a surprise runner in the Casanova Stakes. Yet it transpired that he was an expert seducer of women such as Aileen, to whom he gave the full force of his sympathy and attention, while wearing the innocent mask of his physical plainness. Even the two wise women in the kitchen had been foxed by outward appearances. As my grandmother put it, savouring the vivd real-time proof of her remark: 'It's never the ones you think.' Aileen and her beau returned the following night, as if nothing had happened. Nobody said anything (everything having already been said).

This event, and the elements thereof – the astonishingly loud thud, the extraordinary sight of the large barmaid reclining and flailing on the bonnet, the amazement of the onlookers at the door, the greater amazement at how nobody had noticed this love affair under their very noses, the jokes about the car coming off worse in the slow-motion collision… all this became part of the pub mythology. So too did another event, which took place one early evening around the same time. A woman who was not a regular, but who visited regularly (these were different things), had swept in at speed and driven her car too far down the slope: it had hopped over the small stone wall that separated the car park from the orchard, and its front wheels were now poised neatly above the grass, like a cat over its feeding bowl. The fact that the car was hanging in a mere few inches of nothingness only served to mock the situation. It was utterly immovable, and the woman completely hysterical. As she was obliged to confess to my grandmother, choking and retching over every word, the man with whom she spent these regular early evenings at the pub was not her husband. He was, in fact, her lover. Her alibi was her son, who at that very moment was attending his Boy Scouts meeting nearby; unless she picked him up within the next hour the whole structure of her life would collapse; and all because in her excitement, or guilt, or sheer la-la-la-singing-along-to-ABBA thoughtlessness, she had forgotten for a moment to put her foot on the brake.

My grandmother, stern but uncritical, became magnificent. She pulled the woman together with brandy (not Rémy) and exhorted every strong man in the pub to get out there and lift the bloody car. It took a long time. The lover was not among the party: 'He was orf, boyfriend.' Nor was the woman herself ever seen again, after she revved away to the blissful dib-dib innocence of the Scouts' meeting. But the night when this unnamed, unknown person drove over the edge of the car park went down in the annals, along with the night when Aileen threw herself at the windscreen, and the night when my grandmother's old suitor came prancing into the pub ('oh fuck') then crashed his car, and the night when one of the farmers had a fight outside with one of the town men (cause unknown; neither was hurt; afterwards they became the best of friends: all rather *Women in Love*), and the night when a very handsome regular, silently acknowledged as paramour of one of the town wives, was seen outside behind the cellar in a compromising embrace with the woman's mother, and the night when old so-and-so fell in the fireplace and hit his head on a cauldron but was sufficiently drunk to use it as a perfectly acceptable alternative pillow, and the night when everybody had New Year's hangovers, fit to die, but bugger me if they didn't get started again... This was the oral history that is shared by all the people who went to the pub, and that is still occasionally retold, as if in affirmation of the fact that *we were there*, or *we were part of something*, or *we were alive...*

Of course it was hallowed in retrospect. That is the function of collective memory, to endorse and enlarge, to encourage the communal spirit to sing. That is what the women were doing around the solo table, with their 'do you remembers' crooned into the dying Sunday light. Yet if the memories were false – because what memories are not? – they were also intrinsically true. Later I myself – for a very brief span – became part of the nights at the pub; I was there when some unexpected moment, some here-and-now explosion of humanity, held us all in its thrall. And I felt the joy of actuality, of there-ness: a heightened little flare of life. In so far as it is possible, a proper pub is where one lives in the present tense. Today, all too often, there is no present-tense living except in the act of recording it. Everything else is anticipating what will happen ('It's going to be so amazing') and recalling what happened ('Wasn't it amazing?'). What comes in between is as nothing against those two monoliths; it might just as well never have happened, although social media bears witness to the fact that it did.

Perhaps that is why alcohol, rather than pubs, has now acquired such significance, because drinking allows us to sidestep the problem of how to *be*. In a proper pub, drink is central but not all. Today, too many 'do you remembers' are about the times 'when we all got slaughtered – oh, it was great, it was blinding': false memories, despite the indelible screen testimony, because if drink is an end in itself then the beginning and middle have no value, and nothing is being recalled except the fact of drunkenness.

Pub 'do you remembers' are immeasurably different. Their unreliability holds a tender weight, a creativity and a mystery. Alcohol moulds these memories, but it does not make them: it is the pub that makes them, with its lambent and forgiving atmosphere, which echoes and blesses the mellow loosening that comes with drink. *That* is what I – we – are remembering, a particular quality in the light and the air, both magical and human. In fact, the stories that I recall, these absurd little moments of *faiblesse* and folly, are all about the same thing: the warm flame that surrounded them, that beautified them, that honestly made life worth living.

Back in childhood, back in the sitting room, I sensed as at a great distance the world beyond the wooden door. I watched *Top of the Pops* and fondled the tennis-ball heads of the chihuahuas as the headlamps of cars entering the pub threw an intermittent yellow-pink flare across our cocooned comfort. At this hour I would normally have been reading, or doing homework, but such earnest activities seemed irrelevant in this little arena; I could almost hear the joshing, explosive 'What the bloody hell are you up to there, girl?' from the customers. At the pub, even at such a young age, I took on something of their casting-care-to-the-winds attitude. Now was what mattered, the everyday miracle of now. Tomorrow and its reckoning (hangovers; school) existed in another dimension. In this spirit I dined off Quality Street and, from the age of about eleven, lit an occasional experimental Dunhill from the silver cigarette box. If my grandmother noticed, she didn't bat an eye: she was very pro-smoking.

From time to time she would put a bright, Elnetted head around the door (oh, the pistol-shot crack of that handle, I can hear it still) and check that I was 'all right'. If she was bored, if the pub was still in that effortful state in which alcohol was a drip-feed into the communal vein, and every imbecile remark, every 'aah' and 'ah, well' and 'anyway' resounded for long minutes in the near-silence, she might linger in the sitting room; not entirely relaxed, more as if waiting semi-energised in the wings. I became a quasi-customer with whom she rehearsed her part. She would pad lightly to and from the kitchen, offering sandwiches, heaping chocolate fingers on to a plate like firewood (so unlike the regimented rows at the homes of my school friends). If her attention was caught by *Top of the Pops*, she would respond in her characteristic way, in language that I didn't always understand but found gloriously satisfying to the ear. 'Clock the syrup,' for instance, to Alvin Stardust (syrup of figs = wig); or her usual '*Saucebox,*' to David Essex (a derivation from 'saucy,' meaning sexy in a self-conscious and slightly ridiculous way); or 'That old Suzi Cointreau?' to Suzi Quatro (this was a genuine slip, she didn't make jokes of that kind). Most of what we watched was rendered deliciously substandard by her sharp and casual gaze, although she loved Mick Jagger, David Bowie, people who caught the light like the Hollywood stars of her youth. She was not a worshipper, but as a charismatic person she was naturally drawn to those whose charisma had been deified.

When she opened the door to go back to the pub, the noise came in like a suddenly released stream. Then – door shut – it settled into a distant, underwater gabble. My attention was always half upon it; the television could not compete. I became instinctively skilled in tracing the development of the evening, the gradual gathering together of speed and sound and rhythm – headlamps, footsteps, door latch, till ring, laughter – and at last the connection made, the throb of an independent pulse. From my listening post on the sofa this process had an inevitability, like a litany or a love affair, although to the people in the pub it doubtless felt willed and contingent.

From time to time they came crashing backstage to use the phone, almost always the younger townspeople, importing a smell of cologne plus spirits that struck the senses as fiercely as an uppercut. They seemed like lumbering giants as they stooped to stroke the dogs ('All right, little boys?') and perched on the edge of my grandmother's armchair, dialling purposefully, the men in their open shirts beneath suave jackets, the women waggling Dolcis shoes at the end of neatly crossed ankles. Their amiable tipsiness, the imperfect volume control of their voices, made the sitting room feel as unsteady as a ship's cabin. I was very aware of the fact that here were the originals of the kitchen conversations. It was almost like being in the presence of celebrity. There was the same sense of duality, that these were people like anybody else, who could nonetheless generate such myths and fables.

Occasionally, I might go into the bar and summon one of these people to the telephone (no mobiles then; it hardly needs saying, but imagine it). This didn't happen when I was very young; somehow I must have been protected from it. But from the age of about twelve I would have done it. It created in me an irritable panic, because I never quite understood the barking, crackling person on the phone ('Mike in tonight, love? Tell him Mike wants a word') and I didn't know the Mikes from the Bobs from the Steves, they all sort of looked the same and had the same way of talking, like chuckling Saturday-night comedians telling the same innuendo-filled joke that stopped at the salient word, and I dreaded their inability to behave in a straightforward manner. However much I told myself that winks and eyebrow-dances and twinkles were all part of the pub, and therefore to be welcomed, or at least borne, in my grandmother's friendly if mysteriously dismissive way. I was *not* yet part of the pub and therefore found them excruciating, particularly when dressed (as I usually would have been) in my ultra-prim gingham school uniform.

And yet: more interesting emotions lay beneath these girlish embarrassments. For instance I had a certain arrogance about my protected status at the pub; however much I didn't want to go into the bars, I enjoyed the knowledge that I could, that as 'Vi's granddaughter' the entire place was mine to roam. I was full of the sense of being coolly placed at the centre of a world that, to so many of the customers, was the centre of their world.

There was also, most powerfully and alarmingly, an extreme *excitement* about entering the pub at the height of the evening: plunging onstage, a non-actor shoved into a crowd scene in a semi-lawless urban comedy – Jonsonian perhaps, with a Jacobean edge of threat – angling and twisting through the mass of people, whose arms flashed across the bar like swords and who shouldered between each other in that richly impersonal pub contact; feeling the sudden rough clasp of smoke, the steaming walls of flesh, the red warmth pierced by pinpoints and starbursts... It was so *complete*. The difference between this and the sitting room really was elemental, like the sharp dive from shore to sea: not exactly enjoyable, but still a strange kind of physical privilege, an experience that I would not have wanted to miss. The level of turbulence in the atmosphere depended, I now realise, on whether my grandmother was visibly in charge. If I could see her at the shining head of events, an earthy, swooning kindliness prevailed; if she had been absorbed into the evening, it felt harder, coarser. But certain things never changed.

What I saw was not exactly glamorous, nor romantic. I had an image of adulthood – an ideal formed from the Crush Bar at the Royal Opera House – in which people were careful with themselves, held themselves at acute angles of sophistication, laughed in descending arpeggios at nothing overmuch, kept their necks swan-arched and their instincts under civilised wraps. The pub in full bloom was the obverse. It created nothing to which I aspired, but something that I nonetheless found as mightily compelling as thunder. Here, I recognised, was pleasure, so absorbing that people were scarcely self-conscious at all. No imaginary camera hovered to guide their movements. Their contact with each other, even when the pointer of sexual desire fell somewhere in particular, was essentially diffuse and imprecise. Their zest, their vigour, their defiance, was about nothing except itself.

There were some good-looking people among the customers, but by this stage of the evening – a couple of watchful young women aside – that particular awareness had transmuted into something earthier. Faces glistened and crumpled, cotton wrinkled around muscle and gut, crimplene and terylene gave off a telltale hum; none of it mattered. Conversation came in fierce, repetitive bursts, meaningless yet full of its own meaning, in which the country accents sounded like horns interspersed with the thinner, bending notes of urban piccolos. 'What you having…?' (*G and T, just a single…*) 'Better make it a double, he looks a bit thirsty…' 'Go on, get this bugger one 'n' all, he ain't a bad old sort…' 'Don't *want* one? What're you at, man…?' (*Well, all right, one for the road…*) 'Didn't have to twist your arm, did I…' 'No ice? Give him the bucket, girl, let him do a bit of work for once…' Laughter – huge and thunderous surges, exploding into firecrackers of hilarity – had a life of its own, quite independent of whatever remark had caused it. People were drunk, of course, in varying measure, but that was not quite the point. Drink was the enabler, the encourager, the softener. It was the elixir that allowed the pub to work its spell: to become a place where humanity could expand, where everything mattered less and more, where the outside world was kept at bay, where life was bold and safe and affirmed. And fun. That most elusive of qualities, which can be neither predicted nor contrived, which stubbornly refuses to come out to play when everybody most wants it to, but which the pub – not always, but often enough – could coax from its mysterious lair.

Time, too, was different from elsewhere. The subliminal desire for things to be *over*, which afflicts so much of life, was turned on its head. In the pub, people wanted time to go on for ever. They wanted it to be suspended, exquisitely held… and, as the evening got going there arose a poignant, communal belief that this might actually happen, that perhaps time need never move on… Except that nobody really believed it, of course. They knew that time was circumscribed. And in a way they wanted that too, because therein lay the significance of their present-tense living, its depth and texture. So the evening pushed and pulled, pushed and pulled, until the accumulation of noise and energy sounded, from the sitting room, like an organic force, strong and wild enough to transport everybody away from normal life – all those ones-for-the-road became so many what-the-hell ripostes to tomorrow, with its thick-thumbed fumbling for the Alka-Seltzer, its strip-lit grappling with the VAT return, its trolley-pushing round Tesco, its this, its that… How much better to stay here, in this warm-lit room, with the fairy-lit bar, and send everything beyond it up the Swanee! And yet, all the time, the anticipation of the bell, the last round, the encounter with the real and loveless air, and the knowledge that this was as it should be, because it was, after all, a law of nature that the evening's glorified rhythms would lessen and falter, that the state of euphoric mellowness would snap and shrivel, that it is impossible to maintain a continuum of happiness, nor should it be tried – that pleasure is more pleasurable for being framed, legitimised, bounded...

The acceptance of an ending is implicit within the proper pub. There are no delusions of prim immortality. At my grandmother's pub, every sip and inhalation said as much. We are only here for a span.

Nevertheless, the first few rings of the golden bell were ignored. To leave obediently would have been inconceivable, in fact an insult to the pub. Very occasionally a lock-in did take place. I remember being present at one. It was broken up when a sprightly young policewoman stepped into the public bar (a terrible, terrifying sight, akin to the appearance of the Commendatore in *Don Giovanni*) and marched around, on little clockwork legs, asking everybody in a friendly, cheery, ghastly manner what they were doing there. My grandmother dealt with her, and must have convinced her that it was a private party, because the evening continued. But the mood was shaken – the relief that we were not all under arrest held the vibrato of hysteria – and the policewoman became the sole topic of conversation (the general judgment, that she had 'fancied herself', a wobbly, indignant attempt to reassert pub values).

As a child, I was in bed by chucking-out time. Not asleep.

That too would have been inconceivable. From above the public bar, I experienced the pub with such clarity that I could plot the patterns of people's movements: with eyes shut and mind intent, I could trace the precise disintegration of the evening, almost picture the strands detaching themselves from the mass of noise. The crack of the door – a different sound when people were leaving – came with steady and resigned frequency, the laughter in irregular little shudders, shot through occasionally with bravura – I'm not gone yet! A couple of people always chanced their luck ('Go on, stick one more in there'), pushed the evening to its limit. I waited with the same impatience as the landlady for the final lift of the latch and rev of the engine. At last, like the closing of a giant eye, the lights of the pub darkened outside the bedroom window.

Then my grandmother, with an eagle swoop, reclaimed the place. Earlier she would have escorted me to the low camp bed in her room and arranged beside me yet more offerings: Horlicks, *Harper's*, digestives... her generosity was remorseless, her hostess's gift would have exercised itself on an escaped convict ('Now, what are you going to have, sir'). Although the evening was effectively over, she would twist at the sleek gold stick of Estée Lauder and paint her lips at the dressing-table mirror. In apparent contradiction, she would say: 'Drunken buggers, they'll be orf soon.' Sometimes she dissociated herself from the pub. She had created it, but it was not always the creation that she held in her mind (that was the old pub: the template). She disliked drunkenness, despite being the person who facilitated it. Although she worshipped the mellow state, and loved alcohol with a tender and respectful passion – 'Oh, a drink's beautiful' – if drink took over from the pub, she would withdraw. It was a paradox, sort of. As ever, her personality resolved it.

After closing, when the bars were empty but throbbing with echoes, I again pictured what was beneath me. Victor, if he were still on the scene: sitting on the stool next to my grandmother's, smoking his sixtieth untipped Senior Service and contemplating, as if it were a work of art, the brandy glass whose stem lay between the upturned second and third finger of his hand. My grandmother and Irene: collecting glasses in perilously assembled towers, cascading cigarette butts into the little bin, disdainfully crumpling crisp packets tacky with Worcester sauce, floating to and from the kitchen with the dogs at their heels in order to fashion supper. All this was done in a brisk, delicate, almost unconscious way, their heads rising clear above the hands performing their female tasks ('You've got to be a bit of a woman' was one of my grandmother's odd phrases, meaning do these necessary jobs without fuss and with a modicum of style). I can see her hands now, wrinkled and with a couple of heirloom diamond rings wedged deep in her fingers, trimming the crusts from salt-beef sandwiches, quartering tiny tomatoes, making a simple meal into a careless work of art.

Then the spark of the pub was rekindled in her sitting room, in the modulated way that she understood and loved. I knew this, because I would sometimes go down and sit behind the door at the bottom of the little staircase. There was a long crack in the wood, wider in the middle, through which I had a part-view of my grandmother, Irene and Victor, seated on the sofa and armchair, angled around a low table sumptuously weighted with decanters and tumblers. Everything in the pub was about a quality of light. Here it was full, voluptuous, a chequering of heavy gleam and foggy aquamarine. As they painted mustard into their sandwiches with a miniature silver spoon, the three people discussed the evening – 'Christ, did he now'; 'Yes, I *heard* her say that'; 'Bugger me, he must have had a few' – in a way that created a particular weave of sound: Irene's barks, my grandmother's dry responses, Victor's conciliatory mediations. The mood was more judicious and expansive than in the morning kitchen conversations but there were the same ellipses, that same sense of the shared unspoken.

Around and about the conversation was music from the old gramophone beside the fireplace. The dusty buzz of my grandmother's records – still occasionally played – takes me instantly to the last but one step of the tiny staircase. Even if I play the same songs on download, I hear the premonitory dance of needle on vinyl; the sound still comes at me in a remote, mysterious, veiled way. I see again the stacked LPs with their tatty inner sleeves, their worn covers bearing beautified faces, marmoreal and mask-like, from a time when women contained limitless pain within *moiré* and pride. I inhabit that sense of synaesthesia, as curlicues of trumpet wove in and out of trailing smoke. On these private occasions the music was remote and austere: thin threads that pierced the heart and grew inside it. Early Dinah Washington, Billie Holiday, Peggy Lee, the sainted Bessie Smith. Out came the big female phrases, the terrible erotic fatalism:

... St Louis woman with her diamond rings/ She pulls my man around by her apron strings

... Someday, when you grow lonely/ Your heart will break like mine and you'll want me only

... I ain't gonna marry, ain't gonna settle down/ I'm going to drink good moonshine...

Sometimes there would be a short outburst from my grandmother's confident, rather tuneless voice, half-singing half-talking a favoured lyric – '*... ain't got nobody/ And nobody cares for me...*' That was Crosby, worshipped by the women ('He's got dirty eyes'). Victor, meanwhile, was steeped in Bix and Bing, Billie and Lester, Frank and Nelson, in the gorgeous sorrowing yelps of José Feliciano, to whom he introduced my grandmother; as he listened he inclined his head to a particular knowing angle, or flicked at a solitary air guitar string; but he did it with humility. He had the musician's true respect for his own kind. He shared the soundtrack of my grandmother's life; it was a bond that I would later understand, the sense that their ears echoed with the same cadences. And these songs, played at this hour, heard in the hunched darkness of the staircase with its wavering crack of light, seemed like a deeper expression of the pub code, in which everything was known, everything about life and sex and sin – there was nothing that this music didn't know or hadn't seen – and everything was accepted. It was forgiving music: spirit-soaked and slow-smiling and forgiving. In old age, my grandmother (who in her black-haired exotic thirties had looked very much like Billie Holiday) would sit at the kitchen table and listen to the records, her expression oddly wide-eyed, her thoughts a mystery.

She also had a taste for less elevated stuff, unabashed in its punch-the-air climaxes, orchestrated as if in the deep-pink velvet of her bedroom: Brenda Lee, Timi Yuro, tiny women with pulsating diaphragms and a majestic, maudlin sincerity. These records were played when the company was larger, perhaps including the solo school or other favoured customers, all of them crammed into the sitting room, with the dogs' ears quivering as the tight-knit band raised their glasses and begged each other to '*make the wo...rld go away*' or urged themselves '*u-u-up the lazy river...*' 'Lazy River' was anthemic, adored, the pub's song. My grandmother had versions by Bobby Darin and the Mills Brothers, but it was Brenda Lee's sweet little girl's heckle that sent people into a frenzy. Her swooping rises and falls had the sublime cadences of drunkenness. Not even a 33/1 winner could make my father look as happy as the moment before he went up the lazy river, that momentary back-pedal as the horns set the scene for the vocal, the glass raised and then the divine plunge...

There were rogue elements within my grandmother's record collection. Being completely unselfconscious, she simply bought what she liked. Among her battered singles were David Cassidy's 'Daydreamer', Chas and Dave's 'Ain't No Pleasing You', and Barry White's 'You're the First, the Last, My Everything'. She loved Harry Nilsson, and treasured an album in which he covered old standards in his propping-up-the-bar tremble: '*... another bride, another groom, another sunny, honeymoon...*' This was wildly popular at Christmas and New Year's Eve: aged eight I knew every word. On those days of celebration the gramophone was transported into the bar, and the pub became an absolute expression of my grandmother's tough bright soul.

Indeed I have never since known Christmases quite like those at the pub. I remember how, on my return to school in January, my friends at this excitable, ladylike establishment would chatter about church, and presents after lunch, and walks through snow; we were mostly the same kind of girls, privileged little beasts dreaming of dancing Giselle at Covent Garden, yet a different England ran in our separate veins – they had no way of knowing the pictures in my head, of the pub in its proud and gaudy innocence. It was not the whole of my life, nothing like, but it was a backdrop that made me feel luckier than they; I couldn't actually imagine Christmas in a private house. It seemed pallid (still does) unless enclosed within the adult grotto of the pub. The word still conjures green leaves pricked with half-hidden points of light, an immense silver-white tree on the stone flags of the fireplace, baubles of incomparable size and swell, little windows misty with expectation, Johnny Mathis asking if reindeer really know how to fly...

We – my parents and brother and I – spent the whole day there. In the morning was a tumultuous party, at which the air of munificence that my grandmother gave to the most ordinary situations became as thick as golden cloth. Only regulars were welcome, and nobody else came; it was one of the pub's characteristics, for which some people disliked it, that it was able to shut up shop against non-members.

I knew all too well the reality of the preparations behind the party. I was in the kitchen in the morning when the gleaming deposits of caviar were scooped from the floor, almost out of the chihuahuas' mouths; I was in the saloon bar on the dark afternoon in mid-December, listening to the curses – 'sodding vicious bastard stuff' – as the holly refused to be nailed into the ceiling beams. Yet what was created was a concentration of magic. Of course I was a child, and illusion was what I dealt in. But then so too did the pub. I don't think I am misremembering it.

The party was a ritualistic affair: every year the same, every year another accretion of familiarity. The tables in front of the settles were covered with a Stilton, a ham, a pork pie the size of a wheel, vol-au-vents that bloomed and shed their hot petals. My father made a champagne punch, thick with slices of orange, to which (as he knew she would) my grandmother added great surreptitious glugs of brandy. Ladled into silver goblets it looked merely festive, beaded daintily with bubbles, but it was completely lethal. The customers barged and roared, their bodies locked together in a mosh pit of merriment that kept them from falling sideways. Such a party! One could not move, one could scarcely breathe, one's back and arms were pricked with holly, one had to fight and jab in order to get through and replenish the vast plates of food, which were fighting their own battle against the lunch in the violent old oven ('How's Bill doing?' my grandmother would ask as she breezed swiftly through to the kitchen; she meant the turkey. 'Bill' was her generic name for anything male). The party was more than I could deal with as a child, although if sent out on an errand I could wind in and out of people without them knowing I was there, so lost were they in their fierce dedication to pleasure. Returning to the sitting room from the bars, the atmospheric change was so strong that the door in between seemed to fall like a blade. The noise beyond the wooden door had a clogged quality, as if every space and every second had been filled with urgent life.

It was around three o'clock, when the steam from the oven was forming a white mist that drifted into the sitting room, when the last customers would topple out of the pub. From the window I would watch them circling the car park like people lost in an invisible maze (one regular was rumoured to fall in the turkey every year as he stood to carve). But for us, the people in privileged possession, it was the next phase of the pub-hallowed day: the tables were moved to the centre of the saloon bar and I – this was my 'job' – laid out the Royal Albert, the tall wine glasses in different jewel colours, the crackers from Harrods and the candelabras. I see it now, the sparkling profusion and the faces merrily indistinct around it. I recall the splash of Courvoisier over the pudding, the flick of my father's lighter, and then the wavering little blue flame above the pudding, advancing and dancing through the darkened saloon. Cards might follow, or even shove ha'penny, which none of us except my grandmother could play properly; the board had belonged to the old pub. We were kept alert by the knowledge that there would be evening opening, although the assemblage was sparse (in my father's analysis, 'a few old boys who've had a bull-and-a-cow with the wife') and impossible to take seriously. A couple of friends would turn up. Victor, who had spent the day with his son, would good-humouredly man the bar while everybody else was crammed, glass in hand, in front of *Morecambe and Wise*. Certain people at the morning party would have stated, with the unarguable intensity of the drunk, that they would be *back later*. This threat always hung over us, but it never materialised.

Yet the next day the customers had indeed returned: full of febrile hair-of-the-dog energy, darting in and out to watch the racing at Kempton, ready for more of whatever was going. This was aftermath indeed, in which the poor old body exhaled booze at every turn and was slapped and sprayed and trussed into a civilised state, only to be overwhelmed once again. 'What a life, eh'; 'What a bloody shower we are'; 'Ah well, only here once.' In this faux-rueful, in fact wholly unregretful way, Boxing Day also held the essence of the pub: being a reminder of the human necessity of pulling oneself together and going back out there for the second act, because one was a hell of a long time offstage.

Then: the New Year's Eve party, with its exquisitely uncool congas and hokey-cokeys, its *u-uupp* the lazy rivers and Bill Bailey won't you *please* come homes, and incidentally my first proper experience of the evening pub. I was thirteen; I looked older, because I would not have dared show a party face to my grandmother without lipstick, and I was treated with an elaborate and careful gallantry. At some point that same year I had been given my first gin and tonic. I can still picture the tumbler on the counter, the watery gleam of the hammered copper reflected in the glass, the crescent of lemon lounging like an odalisque upon fat cubes of ice. My grandmother would have mixed 'a *good* drink'. I did think it delicious, and told her so, at which she nodded with cursory approval. 'Not like your mother,' she said (it was a family joke that my mother, a lifelong teetotaller, was the black sheep among us). As I recall, it had little effect on my head, although today if I drink gin I am instantly silly. Probably the bracing presence of the landlady impelled me to hold my own. The obligations of the adult pub, which for as long as I could remember I had observed, were beginning to apply. From that first drink I had a vague, cavernous sense of something falling away from me, the afternoons amid the thick blossomy apple trees, the illusion that time was infinitely on my side; I was aware, quite suddenly, of the concept of last orders, in all their necessary laughing tragedy.

In the nature of things, closing came very late on New Year's Eve, so late as to represent a dwindling, rather than the pub's usual fight against the customers' urge to continue. An hour or so previously, the chimes of midnight had been relayed from a stout wireless placed on the saloon bar counter: the solid sound of the pub had momentarily dissolved as a crackle emerged from between the near-silent spaces, blooming into the thick distant roar of Trafalgar Square, where in my other life I had held out a handful of seed for the descending pigeons; and then at the last chime life began again, not exactly renewed but reinvigorated, not with resolutions but with a tatty rendition of 'Auld Lang

Syne' in which my hands were again descended upon: a confusion of indiscriminate intimacy, heightened and encouraged by the pub, whose stone and brick walls held us so firmly.

I recall one New Year's Eve in particular, early in my pub career when I was aged perhaps fifteen. I don't remember anything about the party. It is the breath of aftermath that remains inside me. The gathering had thinned to an irregular circle in the public bar, the barmaid Aileen had stepped outside with a sober goodnight nod ('There goes cheerful Charlie'), and the last headlights had been swallowed into the country darkness. The night hung on its brink, swinging gently by its shortening thread: time passing, time suspended.

From the fireplace, the voice of Peggy Lee trailed its lethal sweetness into the air. Is that all there is, she asked, as her band played its mocking little two-step; to which came no considered reply from her listeners, merely the murmured litany of collective response: Is that all there is? Behind the counter sat Irene, upright on a stool, eating olives and placing the stones on a beer mat. Occasionally she would receive my grandmother's glass of champagne and fill it with a short black stream of Guinness. Her movements had a steady automatic efficiency, which I watched, half-mesmerised, from my low stool beside the fireplace. Otherwise the evening had slowed almost to immobility: people nodded their heads wisely at the music, inhaled and sipped with the air of connoisseurs; the frenzy of earlier consumption was now quietened.

The lights in the bar were very dim. Smoke drifted and spiralled in thin whorls. The atmosphere had mellowed into something soft, full and gold-grey, in which the pub and the people became configurative as a painting.

Who was there? My memory is inexact, as ever looming and receding in its precious way, but I can see the close circle made by the counter, the fireplace and the dark wooden furniture, and within it a few figures: Victor with his West End bravura and new silk tie, eyes half-closed as he mouthed the song quietly and respectfully; my father, wearing his habitual expression of shrewd good humour but with eyes a little widened, relaxation making him look both older and younger; one of the farmers, who had earlier commanded the room by reciting the whole of 'If', and now stood tamed, becalmed, but still eager for whatever snatch of fun might be going; a couple of the townspeople, heads tilted gamely as they sang into each other's faces, the savagery of their life together absorbed into this lax benevolent dusk; my grandmother on her stool, casually nursing the glass that rested on her thigh, her face in enigmatic smiling shadow, her head shining beneath the wall lamp like Lili Marlene.

The moment held an essence both ephemeral and eternal, as all such moments do. Through the amber mist came clarity: a sense of the dying falls that lay within delight, of the terrible poignancy that lay within human beings, and of the stern generosity of the pub in allowing this revelation.

I had had a drink, of course.

'… *a drunk man in a pub who suddenly embraces his neighbour, and then stands drinks all round, is nearer to the truth of things as they really are, to reality, than any thin-lipped puritan will ever be.*'

From *Absolute Hell* by Rodney Ackland

'And is not my hostess of the tavern a most sweet wench?'

Falstaff, from *Henry IV Part 1*

II

My grandmother had to fight hard for her pub. In later life, towards the end of her century, she told me the story, speaking with the honesty that characterised her, as it does all truly confident people (what need to lie, when there is no need for shame or self-doubt?). If she didn't remember something she would say so, and what she did remember was conjured with a soda-stream burst of quick clarity. I enjoyed her relationship with her memories almost as much as the memories themselves. Things were simply as they were, or as they had been, and she seemed amazed that I didn't share the pictures in her head, which to her were as sure and immutable as a line of portraits in a gallery.

She was also surprised that I wanted to have these pictures described to me. She didn't really understand how somebody could be interested in a past that they had not inhabited. She had believed in pub life, 'Oh yes, beautiful': it was, after all, the life in which the rest of life congregated. But it was 'gorn', and like so many of her generation she was an emotional pragmatist (it is we today, dissatisfied within our self-importance, who fetishise the past). Such nostalgia as she felt lay meshed within the voices of Dinah and Peggy and Bessie, to whom she sang, woman to woman, as she cooked her resplendent meals with a wine glass of sherry to hand.

But she liked my interest, of course. Why wouldn't she? So in fits and starts she told me how she had come to the pub in the early 1950s, and what the pub had been like when she arrived there. It was not such a long time ago; nevertheless, the remoteness was humbling. She described a dull-lit, part-coloured world of dishevelment and discomfort, of ashy grates and a single rusting tap, of cold rotting wood in an outside privy, a world deprived not just of the ease that was her natural physical milieu but of the basic post-war amenities.

She told me, too, that there had been no counter to stand behind in the pub. 'Well no, there was nothing there. Just a shelf, you know, for the bottles.' She mentioned this in passing, as if it were again something that I had surely known: yet this one detail, this central absence, was like a symbol of her unreachable past. I couldn't picture the pub without the counter. No, I couldn't see it. The pub, without that complexity of spark and sheen, that absolute of light, that unholy grail? My grandmother with no counter to frame her was like a Mona Lisa unhallowed by da Vinci. My grandmother's pub with no counter was like her face with no lipstick.

In fact counters are a relatively recent development, a nineteenth-century derivation from the long serving bar characteristic of gin houses. They are not necessary, having been conceived simply as an efficient way to handle large numbers of customers. Not necessary, but needed: like the pub itself. They give a pub its shape and heart. They are always, and consolingly, the focus of the eye. They are a stage within a stage, a demarcation zone, an altar, a framing device; a damp and friendly resting place for elbows, glasses, fags; a Rayist painting, a flashing Goncharova, albeit so much more nimble and alive then those studious grids of light on light... 'No *counter?*' I said. 'Well, the brewery got one made, didn't they, sharpish.' My grandmother sighed, smiled. 'You see' – she made an effort, not mental but imaginative, to explain to this person who understood so little and who, for reasons that she did not fully understand, wanted to know more. 'It wasn't really a pub when I went there. It was – what could you say – it was like an inn. But it wasn't even that, really. It was a couple of rooms. It was nothing. To what it became, when you knew it.

'No, I suppose that was my doing.'

Actually she should never even have gone there. The story of why she did so is, again, almost unfeasibly remote, and one that the women of today could rightfully march over (but this is not that kind of story).

When her father died she had sought to take over his licence; to her this was the most natural thing in the world. For the previous ten years she had run the old pub, and she believed that she would continue to do so.

She had become the old pub's *châtelaine* after her mother's death, at the start of the war. Her father was ageing. Her marriage was over before it began (she may have fallen for my grandfather, paying his court to her across the bar, but romantic love was not her thing), having effectively ended when her husband went off to fight. So she lived at the pub, her home, with her daughter, my mother; and she ran the show.

Rather enjoying the potential shock value of this statement, she later pronounced the war to have been the best time of her life. 'Oh, without a doubt.' She had been made for it, with her vigorous stoicism and stalwart glamour, the kind that is almost manly in its swagger; had her talent been slightly differently conceived she would have been out there entertaining the troops, keeping people's hearts up like her beloved Vera Lynn ('wonderful woman'). Instead she celebrated the primacy of pleasure in her own way, maintaining her standards – Max Factored brow, spit-in-the-black mascara, under-the-counter nylons – as two fingers to Hitler. The war magnified her personality, her attitudes. She would have liked the fatalistic good cheer, the jaunty nerviness (too much calm always bored her), the surprise element within customer traffic (a Pole! a GI!), the men keyed up to a pitch of do-or-die flirtatiousness, the human give and take of the black market, the constant sense of an occasion to rise to. She had what she craved – protection and freedom – and she had her pub.

And then, when my great-grandfather died, the brewery would not give her the licence. The reason was very simple: she was a woman. To be accurate, she was a daughter. A wife would have been allowed to take over the pub. But then so too would a son.

I can't quite imagine what my grandmother thought at this point. She made nothing of it in later life – victimhood was not her thing; she would have been far more dramatic about a bad hand at solo. In her shrugging way she accepted the fact that femaleness, so often her trump card, had let her down. Of course she knew this was wrong. She was always on the side of women, and anyway she knew that she was as good at her job as any man (better, was what she really thought). She graciously accepted the vehement outrage that I expressed on her behalf. 'Oh yes, it was a bad thing.' Yet when she uttered throwaway remarks of that kind, which contained so much more than they expressed, I was aware of a depth of experience that I could never plumb; she had fought, truly fought, in a way that I could not grasp, and I was back in the sitting room at the pub, listening to the whispers among the coffee cups, in the unreachable world of the grown-ups. My grandmother was always sceptical, or perhaps realistic, about the sacred notion of equality. To her, gender was a swings and roundabouts issue, and that was something that laws would never change.

The brewery had her straight out of the pub. 'Well, that was their right.' Within the period of a few weeks she had lost her father and her home. And she was a single parent by then: she had divorced just after the war (appearing in court on the same day as the film star Jessie Matthews, who livened proceedings by fainting as her own marriage was severed). Again, she made nothing of the lone mother status, which in those days was not a recognised condition alleviated by governments. She had friends, she had relations, people who joined hands to help her – that was how she saw it, the networks of her life tightening to protect her – but it must have been frightening. Pubs were not merely her life, they were her livelihood. Yet here she was, denied the right to continue in her profession – the only one she knew, at which she was, incidentally, greatly gifted.

What to do, in a country where the hangover of war still hovered and there was no longer a bright-lit bar to make it all better? To be chucked out of a *pub*, that sanctuary, at such a time, was exile indeed.

For a year she camped with one of her brothers (she had five, all older than she; as the last child of a forty-year-old mother she always called herself 'the scrapings of the barrel'). She took her daughter, her black Labrador Ricky, and not much else. Most of the family furniture had to be sold – some wonderful things, hard not to lament: vast mahogany wardrobes fitted out like mini-shops, a lacquered Chinese cabinet that would probably now be worth a fortune. 'Um, but what could you do, going from a great big pub into a room?' The sitting-room piano lodged with Irene, who many years later grudgingly returned it. Also sold were the pub's green leather bucket chairs, deep in their embrace; the gleaming black settles were kept in storage, awaiting a future like my grandmother.

She was vague about how she found this, as always when asked anything too factual. She must have talked to people, bustled hither and thither with her smile lipsticked into place, 'putting herself about' in her own phrase, trusting not in God (she was a militant atheist) but in the rewards that she was surely owed. 'Chin up,' was her mantra, and unlike most philosophies it was one by which she actually lived.

Eventually a big brewery granted her a licence. She was always deeply grateful to them; also to one of her friends, a rich local businessman, who had put in a word for her. Having perceived an injustice, he used his influence to right it. He had no romantic intent (although my grandmother would doubtless have inferred one, had the recipient of his kindness been somebody other than herself), and his disinterested favour may have been the origin of the phrase 'you've got to have a man'. Which in this instance, at that time, was true.

And which makes it all the more intriguing that she did not carry her argument to its logical conclusion, and get married again. Victor had asked her, when she was still running the old pub. He had it all planned out; her acceptance, as he thought, in the bag. He had found a hotel for sale on the south coast (Hove? Worthing? – she couldn't remember); took her down there on an ostensible 'day out' and suggested that they run it together. Recalling this event, she conjured the gesture of Victor's hand sweeping out toward the hotel façade, as one who offered her the world on a piece of Royal Albert, and smiled with a trace of kindly pity in remembrance of his excitement. 'Yes... poor feller.' As far as I could see, she never regretted turning him down, not that she went in for regrets.

She told him that she could not leave her father, that she had to think of her daughter, but it was more complicated than that. She had a calling, which did not involve playing wife to Victor's master hotelier. How surprising it sounds to describe the landlady life in that way. A calling is for nuns, or ballerinas. But something, some unacknowledged desire to be mistress of her own destiny while remaining true to her treasured upbringing, kept her dedicated and self-absorbed.

According to my grandmother's myth, which grew up around her and apparently without her volition, she was the first woman in England to be given a publican's licence in her own right; that is to say, as neither a wife nor a widow. I have found nothing to contradict this story. Beyond doubt she was the first in the area, and as an independent female operator she remained a rarity for years. And what she took on was huge. The first pub that the brewery offered to her was a fairly smart town place, but it had no spirits licence so she turned it down. She was right to do so, although she was also brave. Even she may have doubted herself when she arrived in Victor's Daimler at the little thatched barn that was to become *her* pub and a ring of farmers – faces the colour of beef carpaccio, pint and pipe held aloft in either hand – turned slowly to look at her.

In the memory that she gave to me, the men were gathered on settles around the great fireplace in the saloon bar. That, in former times, was how people had sat in the pub. In the public bar they used a couple of benches, and thickened the sawdust into paste with the muck on their boots. These customers were the fathers, uncles and grandfathers of the country people whom I later knew. Old Gus, old George, old Dick, old Percy. The landlord was among them, also with his pipe and his beer, making semi-conversation. 'Well, he was an old boy, wasn't he.' He was popular enough with the locals but the public aspect of the house had scarcely signified to him. It was a house with an open door through which certain people came in to drink, which is how pubs were, in their earliest incarnation.

Similarly, before the arrival of this landlord, the pub had belonged to a widow who lived there with her daughter. So my grandmother was not the first female to have charge of it, although the set-up could not have been more different. The former landlady had owned the place, with no fear of being thrown out: she was truly in charge in a way that my grandmother could only replicate illusorily. Such was the luck that came with a free house, one of those rare establishments that were not 'tied' to or rented from a brewery. The previous pub's owner was rather well-off, in fact, although she didn't appear to be (unlike my grandmother, who was a great believer in what she called 'swank' and could not possibly have afforded a free house). After selling up to the brewery she remained in the village all her life. 'Nice old lady.' When she had owned the pub it was a home, really, a dusty and hay-strewn country cottage; it had the merest hint of a public dimension. When one of the locals came to visit, the daughter would go down to the cellar – that *oubliette*, with its perilous stone staircase – and fetch up a jug of ale, for which a small amount of money was charged. That was it.

And then: my grandmother. Black-haired, bejewelled, bohemian. Probably resented by the landlord (whose retirement had no doubt been encouraged by the brewery; he could not possibly have made them any money). She had never lived out of a town, and had never been anywhere more rural than Epsom Downs. Moving to the country was almost like emigrating. True, she had a Labrador, as did most of the farmers; but for a somewhat different purpose (keeping camp beds warm rather than retrieving pheasants). One of her first moves was to buy a pair of jodhpurs. As an attempt to fit in, it was uncharacteristic. Her sense of self was essentially unassailable, and it almost immediately began to weave its powerful spell.

But the pub! It was a broken-down stable, apparently semi-refurbished by Barry Bucknell, the celebrity DIY man who in the days before cornice-worship would go on television and speedily hammer plywood over any available period feature. Thus, in the pub, the magnificent splintery old beams were covered beneath layer upon layer of wallpaper: 'this thick', my grandmother told me, holding thumb and forefinger a quadruple whisky apart. Although the saloon fireplace was in use, its public bar equivalent was nailed up behind a fake wall. That is the sort of thing that people then did to these marvellous old buildings.

The beer pumps were beside the walled-up fireplace, spirits stood on a shelf, and bottles were stashed in a shallow cupboard. There were no Ladies' or Gents' loos, just an outside privy. An Anderson shelter still stood in the orchard. A few tumbledown sheds were filled with stock; these were eventually demolished to make the large car park, plus a garage for my grandmother's Beetle. She had no car when she arrived at the pub, as was then the norm (there were fewer than 3 million cars in Britain at that time, less than a tenth of the number today).

The sitting room was uninhabitable, with its hole in the ceiling later filled with the bathroom. Naturally there was no phone. A couple of years on, my grandmother would share a line with the fearsome farmer who banged on the counter with his stick, but before that she had staggered off, on her languid London legs, to the far end of the village, where a solitary telephone box stood opposite the pale grey church. Sheep wandered across her eyeline as she rang the brewery and gave her drinks orders.

Upstairs at the pub, the bedrooms were connected by a low door. There was no landing, and no private staircase. A set of wooden steps in my grandmother's room took her straight down, with an end-of-a-fairground-ride momentum, into the public bar. There was no kitchen.

So the hours of closing time were spent around the gramophone in the saloon, where the black settles from the old pub shone discreetly in the half-light, where hip baths were filled, where the fire was stoked by a brass poker (which my grandmother would – I can't explain this, but I remember it – dip briefly into a glass of Guinness to make the contents sizzle). Meals were cooked on the oven that stood beside the giant fireplace: a remnant of the days when the pub was an inn, providing food and accommodation to travellers. That was its original function. Like so many country pubs it had been a medieval hotel, in this case on the road to London. People could stable their horses, stay the night – in a communal bedroom on the first floor, or perhaps in an outbuilding. Some 400 years later, when horse travel – or, by then, coach-and-horse travel – was rendered obsolete by the railways, that purpose was lost and my grandmother's pub retreated from the main stage. It became enfolded within the calm rhythms of the rural seasons, of days measured by the sun; its customers were people who lived and died within walking distance of their 'local'.

The pub always had the air of being part of the landscape. A photograph from the late-Victorian era shows it also as part of the village, a little house like any other except for its quarter-open door, which even in that primitive form hinted at the eternal invitation of the pub: the shadowy triangle, glinting with motes of daylight, leading to a ruby-dark interior and the promise of kindly transgression. The building was brick-faced in those days, the white stone of my grandmother's time a distant decorative dream. A low fence separated it from the winding lane – later the road – along which skipped a carefree quartet of Tess Durbeyfields in smocks and caps, village girl contemporaries of the lady who later sold the pub to the brewery. She was recorded as living there in the 1920s. A valuer wrote an assessment, describing 'poor accommodation', a kitchen-cum-scullery on the site of my grandmother's sitting room, and three unused pigsties. Trade was listed as three-quarters of a barrel of beer every week. One bottle of spirits was sold in four months (four hours was nearer the mark in my grandmother's heyday). A final drifting question was attached to the valuer's report: 'Does a little trade in teas?' Thus an image is conjured of the countrywoman and her daughter, collecting blackberries in the orchard, bubbling and steaming them into jam in the tiny space that was later filled with the smells of Rémy Martin and Players' untipped.

It occurs to me now that my grandmother loved luxury so passionately because of her sudden exile to the semi-derelict pub. She had always been adored, treasured, the sleek little girl protected by her brothers and her counter. Then this? 'Yes, it wasn't much.' But her powerful pride forbade her to dwell on the realities of life without a bathroom; she didn't like me to think of her as deserving of sympathy. 'They did it up, you know! It wasn't like that for long.' The brewery had seen the potential – both in the pub and its landlady – and it made wonderfully quick improvements. A gang of London builders lived in the orchard, in a hut that they built for themselves then demolished. Such was the rightness of what they achieved, it was as if it had been that way for ever. Of course the essence of the place – the tiny windows cut pertly into the thatch, the low ceilings beneath which everybody except my grandmother stooped, the rooms shaped like tiny jewel boxes – was truly and richly old. Much of what was done was restoration, the ripping away of those layers of insulting concealment, the emergence of the beams, the interior walls of brick and stone.

But what really changed is that a pub was created. It became a place within which my grandmother could conjure her spells, like a coolly benevolent shaman. A different kind of house: a public house, which to her meant home.

Quite soon the pub was deemed so perfectly pub-like as to feature in a television advert for Mackeson. The film crew employed a stunt landlady, more fool them (naturally my grandmother had primped herself in readiness – 'but they only wanted old Rick': the advert included a shot of the dog trotting across the car park). Later the pub was used periodically as a location, either for itself or for the ancient woodland beyond. In the 1960s Peter O'Toole filmed there. A photo shows him leaning against the counter, fag held close to his exquisitely concave chest, brandy glass in hand, graceful profile sketched upon the familiar old wall – naturally my grandmother loved him. 'Oh gorgeous man.' But in the beginning there was Mackeson, and the sight of the pub emerging, aerial position permitting, from the crumbly black-and-white screen of the television, bought like so many for the Coronation and still holding something of the miraculous about it. To my grandmother, who always loved television, it represented respite. In the early years of the pub she sat watching it in the dim afternoons, her feet soaking in a washing-up bowl full of Epsom salts, easing the effects of the hours behind her new counter. She was up and running by then, the mid-fifties. She made money, although she was never good at saving. She thought it mean-spirited. Whereas her father had put his surplus earnings into jewellery, my grandmother simply wore her inherited rings and spent with the particular exhilaration of one who has truly earned their fortune. She spent on her daughter, of course, who was educated to a level considerably higher than her own (she shrugged away her lack of learning – which did seem to have left uncluttered the paths of her innate sense – but she was determined that my mother's schooling should be different). A couple of years after the Beetle car, she traded up to a Karmann Ghia. She had a mink, as people did, into whose capacious pockets she would occasionally stuff her brassiere on evenings out, having removed it in the Ladies' when she grew bored with wearing it. She had her hair done in Knightsbridge by 'Mr Teasy Weasy' Raymond; she owned clothes by Dior and Balmain; she took the first of several holidays in her beloved south of France, where she drank Campari in the Negresco's ruinous bar. The mystery is that none of this ever seemed incongruous at her little pub. She, and it, met halfway, achieving not compromise but something larger and better.

How did she pull it off? How did she turn a down-at-heel country inn into an establishment so vital, so essentially pub-like, that its legend still reverberates? How was it that just a couple of years after her sudden exile, the pub had become a place to go, a 'bit of a thing', renowned for miles around?

She had help: from the brewery, which knew what it was doing; from Victor, in his semi-detached way, and later from Irene; from barmaids, some better than others; from the friends and relations who came in the early days, and lit up the place with their workaday resplendence; from the customers at the old pub, who arrived en masse in a hired coach to give their support. But the triumph was hers, no question. She did not offer any theory as to how she did it, and she was certainly not interested in self-glorification. She had done it for her daughter – there was a fierce attachment between them, although she was not a 'maternal' woman – and she had done it for herself. Actually she had done what she had to do.

How fortunate she was, to lack introspection! What use, after all, is such a quality to a great landlady? No more than to one of the theatrical turns, the old-style purveyors of shimmer and stardust, whom she so much resembled. Just as they, the Hermiones and the Gerties, commanded the Palladium or Ciro's or the Talk of the Town, so she imprinted the pub with her personality: she was not an artist, but something of the same magic was at work. Therein lay her success, defiant in the last resort of analysis.

Personality is one of the few mysteries left to us. It is a beautiful thing, the divine spark of honest self, which in some people is written in italics – as an ineffable largesse, a bright resolution of complexities. And it is all the more precious because it is now hard to find. Facsimiles abound, but we are so self-conscious, so afraid of judgment; and our proclamation of the right to be 'ourselves' is oddly timid, beneath its vehemence, so in thrall is it to contemporary orthodoxy. This is another reason why we are so beguiled by the past: its different freedoms. My grandmother was free in a way that I am not, just as she was constrained as I am not. She was self-absorbed, right enough, but in another way she never gave herself a thought. Imagine that today. She simply lived, covered the expanse of her life without heed and hesitation. Fear did not occur to her. What was there to be frightened of? No culture of constant criticism, that's for sure. You did your best, and people liked you, and if they didn't they could sod orf.

She was inestimably lucky, because her personality found its perfect expression in her way of life. That is very rare; now as well as then. And perhaps it was a good thing that she had to start all over again. The old pub was a known quantity: she and it were as one, comfortable as a married couple. When she moved she had to recreate it, which in the end meant sparking the creation of something new. The pub to which she moved was a force of its own, a different theatre with a different audience: it had to be reckoned with. What she made of it, as she breezed through the little bars in all her capable glory, turning on the lights, the music, the tabernacle flame, was a life's work indeed.

I wonder now if she ever contemplated failure. Practically speaking, it had been far more likely. The early years of the pub were before car travel as a matter of course (oh, the carefree years between the Beetle and the breathalyser), which meant that people had to walk to the pub, either out of desire or necessity; and walk to *that* pub, rather than the rival establishment at the other end of the village, where they could easily have gone. There could have been parochial ill feeling towards this newcomer, this divorcée and single mother with the painted nails and the flash urban ways. A couple of years later the townspeople would come, houses would be built along the village road, but at the start my grandmother was stranded among the farmers: Flora Poste with a large gin and vermouth in her hand.

Yet the country people liked her. They had liked the landlord who preceded her, because he was an old boy and they didn't have to worry about him, but they liked her more, because they recognised qualities in her that went beyond the wearing of jodhpurs. They were on her side. She had changed her home, but she remained in her element.

She was a landlady, the real thing. As such the pub instinctively embraced her. 'Um... well, I was a bit of a novelty. A woman in charge. Not bad looking, I suppose. People came to see me, type of thing.' That was my grandmother's idiom, and on the simplest level it was quite true that being a land*lady* was her weapon. The trump card of her femaleness was restored to her. Word gradually got around that this glamorous creature was running her own show, not half a bad show, and people came to see her doing it; thus her clientele grew. Does this seem unbelievable today? Not really, if one is honest. Should it? No. It is the way of the world. My grandmother knew as much. She accepted it and was amused by it. She turned it to her advantage without hurting anybody, including herself, which is as good a way as any of being a woman.

But there was more. She was moving into her prime as a landlady, and as such, like all proper publicans, she touched a deep and peculiarly English nerve.

Of course pubs are not solely English. The whole of Britain and Ireland has a love for them, and they have been exported, theme-park style, to the streets of New York and the beaches of Málaga. However, it is the English who particularly crave them. The pub is – or was – a delicate reflection of our national character: the stoical humour, the craving for clannishness, the relish for a downbeat kind of glamour, the jokey attitude to sin, the sentimentality, the rebellious obeisance and the fleeting aggression.

The publican, meanwhile, is – or was – the presiding presence, the orchestra leader and impresario: setting the tone then setting people free. In the days before pub managers and chains, the days when a pub stood quite naturally at the centre of its community, a publican had power. From the moment of entering an establishment, a customer was aware of the atmosphere that was being created.

This was not always comfortable or pleasant; pubs are more complicated than that. The lesser publicans thrived on their power, to the point where they might lose sight of the fact that they were supposed to be attracting and serving people – as with 'Tarc' (Tarquin), landlord of The Bible in Kingsley Amis's *The Old Devils*, an exquisite example of the power-crazed publican who, having wilfully lost the sense of how to be normal, veers unaccountably between looking as though 'he had suffered a bereavement earlier that morning' and suddenly becoming 'almost friendly for a moment'. 'Dear, dear, there's a character,' says one of Tarc's regulars, which, of course, is the aim of the lesser publican. To be, in some way, a character: a deliberate oddball, an 'old sod', a bestower of capricious bonhomie or a theatrical misery-guts, a dictatorial creator of darts leagues or domino schools, a wayward waistcoat-wearer, a decorator of the bar with a personal obsession such as angling trophies or Scottie dog figurines or Leyton Orient memorabilia... or some other variation upon an essentially bullying theme, to which a surprising number of customers respond with hysterical delight ('Did you hear what the old sod said to me last night? Ha ha ha...').

The Coach and Horses in Soho's Greek Street made a selling point of Norman Balon, the 'rudest landlord in

London', with his whimsical chuckings-out and sneering refusal to meet the plaintive eye of the drink-orderer. Soho is a little different, of course. Staginess, in whatever form, is pretty much required behaviour. Still, it is the case that being a publican was a perfect potential vocation for a misfit who would otherwise have nobody to speak to: there is a paradox inherent within the job, which is that it can be carried out with some success by a person who is socially inadequate. The bar provides a safety zone, and the customers – whose natural urge is to be 'in with' their landlord – do all the work.

There was just such a publican in my extended family. He ran a country pub (until forced out by the gargantuan rent increases of the 1990s) and was greeted quite openly by all the customers as Moss, as in Miserable/Mean Old Sod. He stood at one end of the bar, jabbering and fretting about depredations to his profits as his charming wife offered an occasional drink on the house. Yet he was, in some way, part of what the customers liked. Had he not been there, grimly selecting accumulators from his *Racing Post* and ignoring people unless they were offering him a Bombay gin ('Eh? Yeeeah… go on then'), the pub would not have been the same. The fact that it would have been nicer is not quite the point. The English love of 'characters' often leads us into these sweetly mistaken identifications, in which a person of dull ghastliness is hallowed for their eccentricity. Perhaps such people make the rest of us feel better by comparison. Perhaps they unite the rest of us in a joke. Perhaps it is simply a national streak of giggly masochism; the French have their rude waiters, but French customers don't *enjoy* their rudeness the way that we do.

Publicans of this kind are absurd but harmless. Unlike the proper publican, they are judgmental, but not in a serious way. There is, however, a more extreme version of the type, whose job is to judge – openly, not secretly – for the express purpose of keeping the pub the way that it is 'supposed' to be: that is to say, free from those whose faces do not fit. Such establishments are not pubs, in the true sense of the term 'public house'. They are meeting places for gangs. Sometimes for actual gangsters (there have been many such, although the most famous will always be the 1960s incarnation of the Blind Beggar on the Whitechapel Road, where Ron Kray shot George Cornell). Or they might be pubs filled with less successful villains, such as the one in which I once unwittingly agreed to wait for a friend, which had a dartboard punctured like St Sebastian and seats with thirty years' worth of ready salted crumbled deep between the cushions, where I was offered a drink by a procession of grinning, snaggle-toothed regulars while the landlord watched inscrutably, as one who had spent his life preparing to deny all knowledge to the police. Or the pub in which the man with whom I was drinking got punched in the Gents' for an alleged slight against Chelsea football team. Or even – a very different beast, yet mysteriously similar – a pub such as the one in a genteel village near my childhood home: from the outside a picture-book idyll, but within a chaos of carved-up little bars filled with ageing twerps in rugby shirts and tight-lipped women like extras from *Midsomer Murders*, where the landlady could shoot death rays even as she served the blood-heat Pinot Grigio...

It is quite usual – traditional, even – for a drinking establishment to regard 'outsiders' as suspect. Ben Jonson wrote that, when an unknown customer entered the Mitre at Cheapside – a tavern, thus a familial precursor of the pub – the regulars would 'all stand up and stare at him, as he were some unknown beast brought out of Africk'. My grandmother's pub was far from guiltless in this regard. It did, frequently, have the aspect of a private members' club. But then a local is always liable to become a club, of sorts. And it *should* have a character of its own, else what is the point of being there rather than anywhere else? It is a question of harmony, of the balance between regular and outsider and publican. In a good pub one does not think about this, one simply gives in to it, yet it is a delicate and intricate thing.

Despite their show of power, the publicans in charge of the most uncomfortably club-like establishments are not, in fact, in charge. They are doing the bidding of their customers, who want the place to themselves. Proper publicans will not quite permit that kind of thing. Naturally they will respect territorial tendencies, the regulars who always take up the same position, and God help the outsider who inadvertently occupies it ('Oh Christ, he's only got old Ivor's seat' – I can still hear Irene's whisper, gleeful with foreboding, as a hapless unknown perched innocently upon a sacred stool). At the same time, the proper publican stands no nonsense. Alongside the deference – to the regulars who take possession of a particular corner of the saloon, to the regulars who play their hands of brag at a particular table, to old Ivor and his seat – there is an understanding of who calls the tune; and when all is said and done it is not the customer, but the publican.

Proper publicans are subtle, smiling creatures. They are far too comfortable being themselves to become 'characters' (occasionally people would call my grandmother a character, which to my mind always implied a lack of worldliness; she was not a character, she had personality). Nor are they interested in playing sadomasochistic games with their customers. Power goes to almost everybody's head in some way, but proper publicans deploy it with the elegance of emperors. They give and withhold, are welcoming yet elusive, warm yet cool. If they put a foot wrong – my grandmother, fondly bestowing the wrong name upon a customer throughout an entire evening – they betray no awareness of it. And they cannot be bought, despite the innumerable, plangent, 'go on *have one*' offers of drinks (my grandmother's chucking of said drinks onto the floor was a further demonstration of power, with which nobody dared to remonstrate). They are controlling libertarians. Figures of authority, authorising pleasure.

This is tremendously important, because the English – of which I am one, therefore 'we' – are not at their best with unregulated pleasure. It goes to our heads. On the whole we do not naturally understand how to enjoy ourselves, nor how to stop when enjoyment is over (I blame the class system: it has dulled the autonomous instinct, and its effects are still with us however much we say otherwise). The glory of the proper pub, with its implicit code emanating from its proper publican, is that it gently solves this existential problem. It gives us what we innately crave: a licence to pleasure.

And when it is a woman issuing that licence, the presiding presence is all the more delicious. Why are pubs in popular culture almost always run by a landlady? By Annie Walker, Jolene Archer, Peggy Mitchell? Because the landlady is better theatre than the landlord. She brings to the role an added dimension and gleam. Power is more fascinating when filtered through femaleness (this may change with time and custom, but by then the landlady will be a long-gone species), when streaked with the possibility of vulnerability. If the little pouter pigeon Peggy threw customers out of her pub, she was being physically courageous. If a hulking great Al Murray does the same thing, he is being a bloke. And there is a further simple ambivalence about the landlady. She has the barely challenged authority that is generally granted to a man, yet she wields it in high female style: with a festive celebration of hyper-womanliness.

The landlady – by which I mean the figure as delineated in popular culture – exhibits a knowing, winking exaggeration of 'female' traits. She wears the equivalent of a uniform, designed to signal either good-natured availability (tight, tinselly) or matronly competence (brisk, bosomy). She listens to men with wry sympathy – the elbow on the counter signifying intimacy with boundaries – and responds with seen-it-all wisdom. She serves, obliges and dispenses. She prides herself on her desirable 'house'. Like the lesser type of landlord, she may exert her power by cheaper means, acting the shrew or the dominatrix, but she remains within the familiar spectrum of feminine roles.

Nor is her power diminished by all this emphatic womanliness. It is underlined. The landlady is following the rules of an old game, and everybody knows it; but it is a game that she herself controls.

So strong is her image that it makes little difference whether or not the real woman resembles it. My grandmother would have dismissed the landlady of popular culture as vaguely insulting (Bet Lynch? *Please*) and, like all concepts, completely irrelevant. She was herself, always and only. But images do not develop in a vacuum. They are informed by observation, however skewed this may become along the way. Because my grandmother was the supreme landlady, she displayed traits that, to the casual eye, would have confirmed the stereotype; and confirmed in turn why the stereotype is based upon truth. She was as colourful as a macaw, and – Bet Lynch again – she favoured leopard print (although it all came from Knightsbridge). She had a hostess's charm, simultaneously meaningful and meaningless ('lovely to *know you*' was her greeting to one and all, pressing the flesh as her eyes deadened with the strain of remembering who the hell they were). She believed unquestioningly in the importance of what she was doing. She commanded adoration and absolute respect, apparently without trying.

And the customers at her new pub – cattle-dealers, butchers, ramblers and the rest – recognised her instinctively for what she was. They were happy, one might even say honoured, to help fulfil her destiny.

It was of course unusual for a woman to wield power and be received without resentment. This is still true, however much we might protest and wish it otherwise.

Yet men, especially English men, especially when they have had a drink, have for many years loved and revered the landlady. She is part mother, part nanny, part sorceress, part goddess. So yes, a fantasy figure – nothing unusual about that – which doesn't mean that the real woman was not equally loved. The insult to my grandmother, chucked out of her father's bar because she was a woman, was committed by the world outside the pub: the customers had not wanted her to go.

In some form or other, the landlady has been with us for a very long time. Her earliest manifestation was as the Anglo Saxon 'ale-wife' – often unmarried, despite the name – who brewed in her home and made a small income from her skill. In the days before clean water, tea and so on, people might drink as much as a gallon of ale per day (even children drank 'small beer'). Brewing – 'tippling', 'tapping' – was a handy trade for a woman, one of the few available to her and imparting a peck of dignity and independence.

The ale was sold either from the woman's home, where she would raise a bush on a pole to advertise its readiness, or in alehouses, which were therefore the first 'pubs' (Ye Olde Fighting Cocks in St Albans is officially the oldest extant pub in England, being an eleventh-century structure on an eighth-century site, but obviously many alehouses predated it). In effect the ale-wife was not so different from my grandmother's female predecessor at the pub, who ran a little home business dispensing alcohol: their tradition lasted a thousand years.

And it survives, in different form, in the 'craft' brew industry. There were women making these in the late fifteenth century, although by then more as a hobby than a living. Throughout the Middle Ages, brewing developed into an industry, which in the nature of things was run by men, and with the arrival of hopped beer in the late fifteenth century the female brewer was almost completely sidelined. The ale-wives at the sharp end were more likely to be working for male brewers or as medieval barmaids ('tapsters'), possibly with a bit of prostitution thrown in. Those who were married or widowed might have charge of a drinking establishment: thus, landladies.

But their status was low, on the whole, because alongside the history of drinking in this country runs a parallel history: that of opposition to drinking. A succession of licensing laws, mostly resisted with roaring rage, were prefigured more than a thousand years ago, by a royal decree issued in 965, which attempted to limit the number of alehouses to one per village, and inevitably failed to do so.

Then came religion, powerfully railing against alcohol as a facilitator of sin. Some truth in that, of course. The proper pub is a counterpart to the church, a place of sanctuary and forgiveness, but drink can be the very devil. I once had a boyfriend to whom a pub was no more or less than a place to assuage a craving, the prettied-up equivalent of a needle full of smack; his forehead bore a constant cold sweat of wine; his urges made me feel, physically, what previously I had merely accepted, the absolute difference between the true pub and alcohol. However, William Langland, in his late-fourteenth-century *Piers Plowman*, conflated the two, just as the Temperance

123

Society hardliners would do some 600 years later. When Langland sends his character Glutton to an alehouse, his fellow customers include tarts, thieves and a hangman, and he drinks so much that he sleeps all through Sunday. Chaucer, in his roughly contemporaneous *Canterbury Tales*, is more urbane, as for instance when one of his pilgrims suggests an alehouse as a venue in which to tell his tale, and the others refuse, on the grounds that only a very off-colour story could possibly be told in such a place. The pilgrim who makes the suggestion is the Pardoner, a man of the cloth. Chaucer was a man of the world, but the Langland view was a force that resounded.

Given that organised religion is rarely a friend to women, it is unsurprising that the ale-wife became a target of this godly wrath, dangerously implicated in the criminal allure of alcohol. She was Eve, the timeless temptress, albeit with a jug of cider rather than an apple in her hand. Some of the medieval ravings against her prefigured the lunacy of the witch-finder. In 1540 the city of Chester banned the sale of ale by any female between fourteen and forty – that is to say, the quasi-official ages of desirability. The conflation of drink and sex; the bullying and terrorised attitudes towards women; the perversely English sense of guilt and concomitant excitable delight in misbehaviour... they are all there.

And yet. The landlady, in the presiding form that we would recognise today – although she no longer really exists – would become a figure who commanded ungrudging respect. What saved and hallowed her was the pub. The easy acceptance of her authority came about when pubs were accepted, with ease, at the heart of our society.

At its best the pub could always cleanse the English of our complexities. Whether to do with sex, guilt, class, lack of confidence, self-consciousness, what you will, they were all let calmly loose and dispersed in the smoky air. The pub allowed us to be ourselves. Therefore we were at home there, quite possibly more so than anywhere else. And for a time – a precious time – our common culture understood the value of this. Of course there were always those who opposed pubs. Yet society, as a whole, implicitly acknowledged the pub's place within it: not exactly necessary, but needed.

When did the pub occupy this position? At a rough estimate, between the ages of Charles Dickens and Tony Blair, peaking between late Queen Victoria and Harold Macmillan.

This is hardly a historian's analysis. Such a thing would be impossible. One can cite facts, yes: about the development of pub counters in the mid-nineteenth century, and the deregulation of licensing hours that so confused pub rhythms in the early twenty-first; about the excitable rush to build pubs at the end of the nineteenth century, and the 'never had it so good' prosperity that began to sideline the pub from the mid-twentieth century.

But my estimate is also about something numinous – an instinct, a hunch. I say Dickens partly in the way that Larkin said that sex began in 1963. It is an imagistic thing. Our image of Dickens is always somehow wrapped in a warm-lit haze, as if seen through a murky, kindly, close-paned pub window. He embodies the pub's earthy, compassionate Englishness, and his characters are repeatedly placed in real-life establishments: the Red Lion at Barnet, where the Artful Dodger took Oliver Twist to breakfast; the George at Southwark, where Sam Weller met Mr Pickwick; the Maypole at Chiswick cited in *Barnaby Rudge* – names and places to evoke a picaresque and freewheeling London, which ran alive with places that were pub-like but not yet quite pubs. In 1812, the year of Dickens' birth, the pub was still evolving from its ancestral strands. By the end of his life, in 1870, it was an entity: officially so. The Wine and Beerhouse Act of the previous year had set out the licensing laws that form the basis of today's system, and that gave the pub its essential aspect of benign authority.

The act was passed a decade or so before my great-grandfather was born, by which time the term 'public house' was widespread. But the foundations for this cultural centrality had been laid beforehand, throughout the mid-nineteenth century, which meant that by 1864 Dickens could conjure in *Our Mutual Friend* the Six Jolly Fellowship Porters on the Thames, a drinking place for the London watermen and a pub in spirit, if not in name, with its 'bar to soften the human breast. The available space in it was not much larger than a hackney-coach; but no one could have wished the bar bigger...' Furthermore it is presided over by a figure of rich, radiant familiarity:

Miss Potterson, sole proprietor and manager of the Fellowship Porters, reigned supreme on her throne, the Bar, and a man must have drunk himself mad drunk indeed if he thought he could contest a point with her.

A landlady, indeed. Not one to arouse the customers' swooning love, but one whose ability to command veneration is beyond any doubt.

Throughout the Dickensian era, drinking establishments were acquiring other recognisable traits: the counter; the separate bars with their different prices and atmospheres; the windows with their soft dimples and fruit-gum colours, their white lettering framed and fretted like ice sculpture; the glow that envelops and hallows. The pub was emerging – it was becoming, as it seemed, what it had always been meant to be. It had evolved from alehouses, taverns and inns, from coffee houses and gin palaces; all of these had aspects of the pub. The alehouse, the oldest of the lot, was about drinking, impure and simple. The inn, fully established by around the late twelfth century, provided food, drink and accommodation. The tavern was for food and drink, possibly including wine, very popular in London from the thirteenth century. These strands were not always distinct from each other – for instance an alehouse might offer some basic food, rather in the manner of my grandmother's giant chunk of Cheddar; a tavern might have a few bedchambers – but the three types of establishment were given separate status in legislation.

They were too as clearly distinguished in people's minds as a gastropub from a Harvester. Alehouses were the bottom of the pile and as unavoidable as rats: at the start of the fourteenth century there were more than 1,300 in the City of London alone, as compared with around 350 taverns, and a 1577 survey of England and Wales recorded more than 14,000 alehouses. Two hundred had been suppressed in London just before this survey was taken: another attempt to do something about drunkenness, and completely hopeless as they continued to proliferate. People wanted them. They were generally small and basic, sometimes barely businesses at all, sometimes brothels on the side. More often than not they were like the worst kind of pubs, in which the desire for alcohol was unclothed by joy and subtlety, and the solace on offer was that of mere oblivion.

Inns, by contrast, stood proud and respectable. They were pub-like in their centrality, not just to their own community but to the life of the nation. Although their first function was as stopping places for travellers, they were often much more besides. Rather like the giant shopping malls of today, which one really need never leave since everything is in them, inns might be post offices, auction houses, holders of goods (some had warehouses in their yards), business centres, employment agencies and places where wages were allocated at 'pay tables'. They might be debating chambers, meeting places for elections or trade associations. They might hold dances, banquets, inquests, cockfights. They might be entertainment venues. By the late sixteenth century it was commonplace to have a 'minstrell' strumming nearby, Wilko Johnson in doublet and hose, while actors flooded into London inn-yards with no doubt the same sweetly annoying zest as today they set up productions of *Huis Clos* in a room above a saloon bar. The more sophisticated rural inns also staged plays, particularly in the seventeenth century, although I doubt that this was the case for my grandmother's pub.

It was only with the advent of the railways, and the death of coach travel – a great national shift that took effect from the 1830s – that the all-purpose primacy of the inn began to fade. Its various functions were dispersed. The first 'station' hotels were built. Some of the major London inns were demolished or – like the Tabard at Southwark, from which Chaucer's pilgrims began their journey to Canterbury – rebuilt in entirely different form but with the same name outrageously attached. Some town inns, reasserting their original purpose, became small hotels. One sees them now on almost every high street, with their wide arches through which coaches entered cobbled courtyards, their solid and self-respecting façades shielding interiors that all too often fail those implied civic standards (bars crowded with ersatz wood, white wine like sugar water, QPR–Wrexham making lacklustre flickers on the big screen).

Meanwhile, country inns retreated, perforce, into the world of their village. Their former occupation was gone. More than a century elapsed between the last stagecoaches and the first steady stream of cars (it was not until the 1960s that customers drove as a matter of course to my grandmother's pub, creating that constant pulsing sweep across the windows). In between times, the country inn was a 'local'. Almost a pub, but not quite; lacking as it did the quality of rogue vitality that gives full value to the words 'public house'.

There is indeed always something urban about the true pub, even when it is situated in the country. That is why its closest spiritual ancestors were those bustling streetwise creations, the tavern and the coffee house. Taverns had the warm ruby glow at their hearts; they conjured that state of alert relaxation, of excitation rooted in the everyday. 'What things have we seen done at the Mermaid,' wrote the playwright Francis Beaumont to Ben Jonson, 'heard words that have been so nimble and so full of subtle flame…'

Of course the Mermaid Tavern had a highly particular clientele, which according to legend included Shakespeare (who, in *Henry IV*, reimagined the real-life Boar's Head at Eastcheap as a literal inn with the fiery benevolence of the tavern and the savage sluttish allure of the alehouse: one would expect no less). Of course there would have been bad taverns, as well as those that were great and good. Nevertheless, when Dr Johnson wrote that 'there is no private house, in which people can enjoy themselves so well, as at a capital tavern', he was precisely elucidating the reason why its descendant, the pub, needed to exist.

Also familiar – as revealed by a seventeenth-century inventory of the Mouthe at Bishopsgate – were the tavern's separate bars: the Percullis, the Pomgrannatt, the Three Tuns, the Vyne and the King's Head, all of them furnished with tables, benches and stools. The Percullis contained an 'oyster table' and a couple of 'playinge tables' for cards, while in the King's Head – more controversially – stood a 'child's stoole'. These places, goes the implication, were for anybody: mostly men but not exclusively so. In that sense they had something in common with the pub of today. So too in the fact that food was there to mitigate the alcohol – in so far as that was possible or desired. Alcohol had a power of its own that no establishment could quite contain, but the vivid natural life of the tavern did its best.

Its hard-edged conviviality was echoed in that creature of the late seventeenth century, the London coffee house. There too one found the mist of mixed breath and smoke and steam, enclosing the clientele in an embrace; there too the sense of liberated belonging, of controlled transgression. In fact, in their earliest days, coffee houses were seen as likely breeding grounds for sedition. Then they became part of society in a way that, again, prefigures the pub. Their interiors – also pub-like – were often shabby, nicotine-shadowed, with sanded wooden floors and tired furniture, but there was a purposeful logic to the décor: everything that was requisite was there, and nothing that was not, and that was how people liked it.

In the same spirit, the coffee house did not demand anything of its customers that they did not want to give. In an atmosphere both energised and unpressurised they could read, smoke, eat sandwiches or muffins, drink not just coffee but tea, chocolate or 'spirituous liquours'. This all-day, all-is-available aspect is again reminiscent of a good contemporary pub; it also sounds like a club, which is what some coffee houses became when they evolved out of existence in the nineteenth century. Before that they were club-*like*, as are so many pubs. Some of them were meeting places for groups of people: Whigs, Tories, lawyers, journalists, politicians, 'stock-jobbers', actors, each set gathering together in its specific coffee house, such as the famous Chapter in Paternoster Row, used by booksellers and writers, in which Charlotte and Emily Brontë stayed on their first visit to London. Charlotte, who beneath her bonneted correctness would have loved pubs, instantly grasped the mysterious joy of being one among her 'pen-driver' kind, and more obscurely her humankind.

The club-like aspect of some coffee houses could doubtless be off-putting to the outsider. They were places where people gossiped, networked, showed off to each other. But they were also places in which people could talk to those who were *not* necessarily like themselves, where they could argue and do that famous thing of 'exchanging ideas', which is rarely as exalted as it sounds but which does, nonetheless, permit the very human desire to express oneself. This kind of congress transferred to pubs. 'Every pub is a parliament', as no less a beer drinker than Nigel Farage has put it; one can make of that what one wishes but the larger point, that a pub became a place where one could talk sense or nonsense with almost complete freedom, is true and important.

More than this, however, coffee houses were places where one could simply *be*, in public. They were 'public houses'. In that sense, they were probably the pub's closest ancestor.

And they were not about getting drunk, although they might be about drinking. So in *that* sense too they resembled an ideal pub, in which alcohol is central, but alcohol for its own sake is not.

At the same time, however, something else was going on, something that came charging in from a wilder but not too distant frontier: the 'Gin Craze'. This was the other side of the story, the untrammelled side, in which the concept of drink for drink's sake was taken to an extreme that might even have defeated the hollering, staggering semi-catatonics of today. Gin! With its wretched allure, like a *femme fatale* dreamed by Baudelaire or the death wish in Billie Holiday's voice... even when gin is tricked out, made cocktail-bar-smart with the jostle of ice, the clean chunk of lime, the plump speared olives; even when it is the tipple of twenty-first-century London youth, sold in faux-apothecary premises and crafted with achingly *recherché* flavourings; still the dip of melancholia lies within every sip. And there was no such paraphernalia in nineteenth-century England. Gin was itself, warm and unashamed and wickedly cheap. It was mothers' ruin, fathers' and children's as well: girls in particular enjoyed the taste. Gin had come to England from the Netherlands, after the Glorious Revolution of 1688 had put a Dutch king on the throne. It was let loose upon the nation by a market that allowed unlicensed production, while other spirits were heavily taxed. Gin was in charge.

By the time the government had understood the implications of this policy, it was too late. The 1736 Gin Act, which put the price up in line with other drinks, led to riots in the streets. People refused to do without their gin and, what a surprise, the black market supplied it. Six years later the new tax had been reduced back to nothing; the craze had to play itself out.

It was, wrote Henry Fielding in 1751, a 'new kind of drunkenness'. People had got drunk all the time before gin arrived, but gin made it so easy. It was as if crack cocaine could be bought at Poundland. It killed thousands of the desperate poor, many of whose bodies were later found to have rib fractures from falling or fighting. A woman strangled her two-year-old daughter in order to strip her of a set of clothes provided by the workhouse; the sale of the clothes fetched 1s 4d, which was spent on gin.

This story is part-reflected in Hogarth's engraving *Gin Lane*. A mother, smiling with a terrible merriment, is shown losing her grip upon a child that will apparently fall to its death. The quality of the woman's drunkenness is indeed, as Fielding suggested, of a new order: *nothing* exists except the lucent trickle in her veins. One does see people drunk like that today, and they are not necessarily poor. Nevertheless, they seek that state. They seek it here, there and everywhere. Not just on nights out, but on trains, at airports, at football matches, on racecourses. It makes no odds where they are, because the desire is to be unaware, to lose the sense of self. The difference between now and then lies in the fact that this condition is sought, perversely, with self-awareness; this gallery is played to even as the gallery becomes a mirage, which the inhabitants of Gin Lane did not think to do. It is the difference, in other words, between having money and having almost none; having a choice and having almost none. Which in a way makes today's drunks, and their urge to get wasted, out of it, done with whatever they are doing, even more wretched than their forebears, who at least had a reason to behave as they did.

Today's drunks operate in a post-pub world. They may do some of their drinking in a pub, but before an outing they can get preloaded on supermarket gear. They can buy cheap booze to be guzzled in whatever private way they choose, just as people did during the mid-eighteenth century, when there were some 17,000 gin shops – many of them former chemists' premises. These proliferated wildly until the 1820s, at which point a measure of licensing control was imposed. The makeshift shops were replaced by an entity similar in its soul, but spectacularly different in its outward show: the gin palace.

One sees gin palaces still, oversized in that grandiloquent nineteenth-century way, towering above the workaday street, dressed up and tough and oddly exciting to behold. Today they might house ordinary pubs. At the time of their creation, they were another step along the road to such pubs, bringing as they did that essential element of the theatrical: with their pediments and columns and gilding, they looked like music hall stately homes. Indeed, music hall itself evolved, in part, from the entertainments that were staged within saloons, which predated gin palaces by a couple of decades. Before they became superior bars – a twentieth-century develpoment – saloons were adjuncts to entrepreneurial drinking establishments, large rooms with an admission fee or higher prices, in which customers could gamble, play a sport such as billiards or see a show of some kind: dancing, singing, comedy, drama. These theatricals eventually became such a feature that they took on a life and identity of their own, but the music hall and the pub remained spiritually allied. They had the same throwaway vigour, the same supremely English mix of sentimentality and lack of sentimentality.

Some forty years before Dickens conjured his proto-pub on the Thames, he wrote in *Sketches by Boz* about a visit to a gin palace. He described emerging from the dark slummy streets around Drury Lane and being transported, almost knocked out, by the sight of a building where 'all is light and brilliancy'. Of course gin-palaces were rough houses, vulgar and decadent and the rest of it. But who could blame people for liking them? I would have liked them. They were literal beacons, places in which alcohol – although still a near-necessity – was associated with something more than just itself, set within a dreamscape powered by gaslight and vitality. They were nakedly commercial, full of advertisements for 'the only real brandy in London' or 'the famous cordial, medicated gin', but that too gave them a lurid beckoning zest. Their popularity was not unlike that of the dog track, which took possession of many cities a century later, and which similarly lifted the working man's soul with its creamy floodlights and its implicit gift of hope.

From the gin palace came that fundamental element to the pub: the counter. In Dickens' sketch, 'two showily dressed damsels' stand framed behind it, barmaids in all but name, watched in awe by 'two old washerwomen' who sit on a bench drinking gin and peppermint (a ghastly concoction whose popularity recurred between the wars). The gin palace counter was made, customarily, of highly polished mahogany. Fittings in dark, swelling wood, interspersed with etched glass, were typical and again inherited by the pub. So too was the use of light: the gin palace created its allure with glass and mirrors, which it deployed like flashing weapons. In the pub this incandescence would be softened and modulated, given areas of shadow and occlusion. Its stage set was a subtle business, whereas the gin palace made no bones about the effects it sought to create.

And what it lacked – not that it cared – was the sense of belonging, of ease. There are several ways of behaving when one is drunk, and to a considerable extent these are influenced by where one is at the time. Just as the true pub atmosphere induces mellowness, so this unnatural brilliant bombast seems to have sent people into a state of semi-hysteria. Fights were commonplace, as they are in today's oversized, loveless pubs. Dickens' sketch ends with the police being summoned to a mass brawl (if this was an exaggeration, it was credibly so). He also gives a faintly threatening edge to the relationship between male customers and female drink-servers. The respect paid is of the dangerously dashing, 'devil take ye' kind. Gallantry is flourished like a glinting sword; the girls' coquetry is necessarily a shield.

Most striking, however, is the reference to 'the throng of men, women, and children'. At the age of twelve, Dickens himself ordered a 'best ale' – known as Genuine Stunning, a name to conjure with – in an establishment on Parliament Street, but the Drury Lane gin palace was truly no place for children. He also noted, at the end of the evening, the 'two or three occasional stragglers' still haunting the place, 'cold, wretched-looking creatures, in the last stage of emaciation and disease.' However palatial the *mise-en-scène*, the gin endgame remained the same. An air of regret often hovers over closing time, as the light flares into reality and the evening is dispelled into nothingness. But what Dickens described, because it was about drink as the only succour, was of a different order. Those who wrung their hands and decried alcohol as the root of all evil should, perhaps, have turned their argument on its head: the evil was there already, and the alcohol was merely the panacea.

Yet there was, by this time, a rival to the gin palace, offering a better, simpler and kindlier place for it. A place for wholesome and merry boozing, not the insidious kind that wound its way through people's innards, or so Hogarth suggested in *Beer Street*, his companion engraving to *Gin Lane*. The 'beer house' was licensed by the 1830 Beer Act: it was a rare piece of realistic legislation, designed to help people enjoy alcohol without killing themselves, or indeed each other.

Notwithstanding the gin craze, beer or ale continued to be drunk regularly, and brewing had become a big industry: there were twelve major brewers in London, with splendid premises. Whitbread's was said to have buildings 'higher than a church'. The dray horses plodded nobly through the streets, delivering barrels as they would continue to do for more than another century: the sight of these animals, the patient stop-start of their hooves, the steam rising from their haunches into the London air, was one of my grandmother's earliest memories.

What is remarkable, and rather droll, about the beer house is that it bore such a strong resemblance to the Anglo-Saxon alehouse. It was a house, selling beer, quite possibly made on site by an ale-wife, or indeed husband. Spirits were *not* for sale. This was all about knocking spirits off their perch. Later they reappeared – although not in the first pub that my grandmother was offered, which had no spirits licence. As late as the 1950s, therefore, a version of the beer house was still around, although it had in the main evolved out of existence by the end of the nineteenth century. It had either died, or thrived and expanded to the point where it became a truly public house: a pub.

Before that time, the beer house had proliferated to the point where there were around 50,000 in operation by the end of the 1830s, and even these relatively harmless establishments had to be brought into line. Ah, the English and their irrepressible boozing! The Sale of Beer Act in 1854 was a piece of silly legislation, an attempt to reduce Sunday drinking, which led to the usual mayhem and had to be repealed. The 1869 Wine and Beerhouse Act showed more sense. Although not everybody liked it, they accepted it. It prevented the creation of more beer houses, but it did not – as bad laws do – expect human nature to change, just because it said so. Instead it strengthened the licensing laws, thus supplying a sort of framework to drinking, which it turned out was what most people actually wanted: the quality of *authorised pleasure* that makes the pub what it is.

Beer houses, gin houses, ale houses… they had all played their part in the creation of the pub, and now they were all pubs in the eyes of the law; that is to say, they were subject to the same jurisdiction, which, when it came to alcohol, was always liable to be flouted, but which was nonetheless necessary. Licences became a thing worth having, issued only to people deemed sufficiently respectable, often former members of the military. They were not to be risked by allowing gambling, or prostitution, or extreme drunkenness on the premises. Of course these things still went on. My great-grandfather's pub had a bookie's runner called Woodbine Minnie and a couple of semi-resident tarts called Queenie and Nell. They were facts of life, and the pub has always accepted those, but they were not to be waved like banners. Similarly: drunkenness would be forgiven, up to a point, but it would not be indulged. Standards were all, however much fun it was to chafe against them, and the power to maintain them was now invested, officially, in that high priest with the drink-damp stole over his shoulder, the publican.

My great-grandfather was born into this land of pubs. It suited him. Very much like his daughter – lacking only the drama of her physical glamour – he was entirely fitted for this vocation, alight with elusive charm, disseminating his personality with apparent nonchalance, but in fact (like a chef with his seasoning) with an innate sense of how much to give. A tight ring of customers would congregate around him every evening, hoping for more.

He was also a personage within his community. In his interwar heyday, when he had charge of the old pub, he would stroll the streets on his way to his daily cut-throat shave and his smiling importance would be acknowledged on all sides.

The pub was accepted as intrinsic to society, therefore so was he… of course it was not quite that simple. There were still those who opposed pubs, who would have wished away not just the old dives with their watered-down gin and nightly punch-ups, but all pubs, on what they called principle.

To those who view pubs as essentially good, which is not the same as moral, it is possible to see the pub and the church as twin locals. Not so the temperance societies, whose rise was contemporaneous with that of the pub (they originated in Britain in the late 1820s, flourished in the late Victorian and Edwardian eras and faded away, although not completely, in the 1930s). These varied in levels of stridency. Sometimes their warnings were concentrated upon spirits, rather than wine and beer, which given the effects of the Gin Craze was not unreasonable. However, the absurdly named 'United Kingdom Alliance' sought to ban the sale of all alcohol (a prohibition bill was actually put to the Commons in 1859, and defeated with the contempt that one might expect). But the general aim was to force the closure of pubs, if not all of them then as many as possible. In the early twentieth century it was believed that there were far more pubs than was necessary – which was probably true, although this was never really a question of necessity.

The temperance movement was usually underpinned by religious conviction and espoused by Nonconformists such as the Methodists and Quakers. There was also a strong political dimension, as in 'temperance Chartism', which sought to free the working class of a potentially debilitating dependency. Again, this was a legitimate point of view. It was quite true that drink could be a wrecker of lives. Yet such was the quality of some of those lives, it could also be argued that drink was the only thing that made them bearable. Take it away, and what exactly was going to replace it? Against the fervent vision of fine clean living was something less ennobling but more generous: the wooden settle in the dim-lit bar, the glass full of amber consolation, the shuffle of the feet on sawdust tacky with spit, the communion as warm and lax as an illicit bed.

G. K. Chesterton, whose socialism was of an anti-statist cast, saw the pub as just such a friend to the people and, furthermore, as an emblem of freedom. As with the old coffee houses, pubs were where anything might be said without inhibition or fear. An attack on the pub was an attack on liberty, goddammit. Nevertheless, the temperance set came close to a remarkable victory in 1908, when the Liberal government – paying a debt to its Nonconformist backers – set out a bill to close around a third of the 'unnecessary' pubs in England and Wales, and to ban Sunday opening in England (this had already happened in Wales, where the ban remained in place until 1961. It was not necessarily observed: a knock at the back door of a pub could open the way to earthly paradise).

This attempt by the Liberals to control drinking, which contained familiar elements mixed to unusual strength, was resisted with comparable ferocity. It was defeated by the Conservatives in the Lords, but before that a rally in Hyde Park had been attended by some 700,000 people, while the Licensed Victuallers' Defence League – that is to say, the brewers – produced clever propaganda, suggesting that shutting pubs on Sundays was unfair to those who could not drink whenever they chose (and, in the case of the prime minister, Lord Asquith, most certainly did). As so often before, the nation's drinkers were making their position extremely clear. Yet the urge to interfere in their habits itched away. George Bernard Shaw, a socialist of very different temper to Chesterton, remained convinced that the public could be purified of its terrible desire for the demon booze. High on teetotalism, backed by those of a similar righteous tendency, he established a community Refreshment Association, offering food and boring beverages. It also sold alcohol (profits to be returned to the association) but in the grudging, guilt-inducing, why-are-you-buying-this manner of supermarkets selling cigarettes: the drink was hidden behind curtains and absurdly expensive. The project failed. It did so in 1913, the year that Chesterton published *The Flying Inn*, a novel set in an England where pubs have been expunged by the ruling Fabians (Shaw and his kind), and a stalwart landlord traverses the country with a barrel of rum and a large cheese, carrying an inn sign bearing the words 'The Old Ship'. A loophole in the law decrees that wherever this man erects his sign, people can come to drink. Thus the pub continues to exist, and to laugh gently at those who would destroy it.

In truth, the enemy was not the pub. In those days it was the nearest gateway to alcohol, and – prefiguring Shaw –

an aristocratic lady of the nineteenth century purged her Welsh estate of all its pubs, thinking thereby to chase drink from the land, and believing quite sincerely that her tenants would be grateful in the end. But the real enemy was lack of moderation, which does not only affect the poor, and does not apply only to drink. And the pub, when it was doing its job, sought to curb and ease immoderation. My great-grandfather's pub stood bang next door to a church, and each temple comfortably accomodated its neighbour. Nevertheless, he was inclined to eject the Salvation Army when it came trooping into his bars. Not just on account of the saintly hypocrisy with which the clear of eye and conscience rattled their tins in the haunt of the devil, but because he believed that he himself made a greater contribution to the public good.

It is precisely that atmosphere of acceptance, not always apparent in the church, that makes the pub so important to the person who has little else. The belief in the perfectibility of life, cleansing the body to cleanse the soul, is with us still, albeit purveyed by lovely millenials wielding a courgette and a spiraliser rather than preachers with eyes full of unworldly sincerity. The pure in heart shall see God; the pure in blood shall be venerated on Instagram and float in a perfect cryogenic eternity. Today's temperance movement includes a religious component, mainly Muslim, but this new secular fanaticism – which seeks to expiate the original sin of physical fallibility – is also helping to condemn the pub to its slow death. In my grandmother's pub, every sip and puff was a shrugging *geste insolente* towards inevitable decline. In moderation, this had its adult dignity. There is very little moderation in the martyrdom of the triathlon and the green juice, nor in the obverse of temperance, the reaction against its insistent call, the wheel-size pizzas and goldfish bowls of wine that torment the body with excess.

And what of the other quest for purification, the one that seeks a society scoured of moral transgression? This too is still with us, although the old sins have been replaced with new orthodoxies. These may have right on the side but, again, they have come to represent a kind of extremism: like the temperance movement, they wish the realities of human nature away, and such immoderation is liable to have immoderate consequences.

There was less of all this in the heyday of the pub. This is not to say that the pub was perfect, but its very imperfection was the point. Louis MacNeice was born (in 1907) into what he called a 'temperance family' and wrote that his father objected to alcohol – and presumably pubs – on the grounds that the drunkard 'loses his self-respect'. To MacNeice, who did not follow the family creed, this 'was all to the drunkard's credit, self-respect being one of the roots of evil'. Even when drinking was not enjoyable, it was 'in a good cause; one was laming and debilitating one's private Satan, one's Tempter, one's self-respect.' By turning the notion of what constitutes 'temptation' on its head, MacNeice exquisitely expresses the point: that there is something humanising, humbling, even righteous in the willingness to shift one's sense of self, and find 'a communion among those whom sobriety divided'.

Thus, in a phrase, the pub is defended. I now realise that what MacNeice describes is what I saw as a child, walking through my grandmother's pub at its ugly-beautiful evening peak. Still, of course, there were those who would not have been persuaded. For the self-respect brigade extended way beyond those who were impelled by religious conviction, into a less elevated and far more common type of puritan: those who opposed pubs on the grounds that they were 'not quite nice'. Or, as the monstrous Mr Thwaites, petty tyrant of the boarding house in Patrick Hamilton's wartime novel *The Slaves of Solitude*, puts it to himself: 'Public houses were not really things which were supposed to take place at all.'

Patrick Hamilton, most of whose books are set in the interwar period, was the great poet of the pub (alongside Kingsley Amis). He was also a great writer about drink: again like Amis. Both men knew of what they wrote, and their characters put it away in quantities to make the head reel, although of the two Hamilton was the heavier drinker. His obsessional style notated the rhythms of drunkenness – every surge and retreat within an evening's session – and the terrible dogged logic that takes possession of the swooning mind. As for pubs, he was alert to every variation on the theme. He knew the provincial businessman's pub with its self-important saloon bar, decorated with coats of arms and creating 'a "baronial" effect of the most painfully false character'. He knew the unpretentious Earl's Court pub, with a canary in its cage and tables covered in green linoleum. He knew the old dive of a Chiswick pub, with oilcloth on the floor and 'a decayed fountain not in use set in a despondent nook'. He knew the workaday Euston Road pub, and indeed made the fictional Midnight Bell the setting for his interwar trilogy *Twenty Thousand Streets Under the Sky*, which my grandmother read as if it were non-fiction, verifying and delighting in every detail of clocks kept fast, horse-brasses polished, early evening bores and so on.

As an English novelist, Hamilton also knew all about class, and wrote about pubs through the prism of his characters' agonised class awareness. Many of them are at home in pubs: like their creator they have that instinct, not just to have a drink, but to step off the street and be instantly absorbed into that other world, that beam-slanted dusk. 'As soon as he got inside a pub tonight, it would be all right,' is what the unhappy, love-tortured George Harvey Bone tells himself in *Hangover Square*. Bone has a quarter-bottle of gin in his own room, and naturally he has a go at that, but it isn't quite the same thing.

Set against the pub, however, is Hamilton's other milieu: the boarding house. Like the pub, it is a home that is not quite a home. At the same time it is the pub's spiritual opposite. Its *métier* is not to forgive but to judge, everything from the timbre of a voice to the loudness of a check suit. Boarding houses were often occupied by MacNeice's 'self-respecting' types – Mr Thwaites being the supreme example – and to such people pubs were faintly shocking, like bookmakers. Accordingly, they had an allure quite disproportionate to their reality. In *Craven House*, also set in a boarding house, one of the residents – a middle-aged husband – regularly dodges the congealing Sunday roast on the pretext of needing a good long 'tramp'; this takes him to several pubs, where he behaves with a wildly inappropriate loucheness that stops him from

147

going off his head. Back among the aspidistras, however, the anti-pub façade must be maintained.

As for women, their response is still more complex, filtered as it is through sex as well as class. Mild, sweet-natured, middle-class Miss Roach, in *The Slaves of Solitude*, willingly sheds the boarding-house sensibility at her local pub not far from London, although she is only emboldened to go there because it is the war, and normal behaviour is suspended. 'She had no longer any fear of entering public houses...' But the Rising Sun is a 'nice' pub, so that is all right. Along with its rather surprising pinball machine, it has the heavily decorated saloon that symbolises decency (it goes without saying that a woman would drink in the saloon). So too does the Friar, the baronial-themed pub in *Mr Stimpson and Mr Gorse*. This, the foremost 'hostelry' in Reading, is where Mrs Plumleigh-Bruce – whose late husband was a colonel, no less – is more than happy to drink gin while being flirted at by affluent businessmen. 'She "detested snobbery" and thought public houses "great fun".' Nevertheless, she is not comfortable with waiting for her man friend while seated alone at the bar. That is not merely losing face, but caste.

The Midnight Bell in *Twenty Thousand Streets* is not a dive. Its clientele contains a very pub-like mix of the educated oddball, the waggish motor trader, the unsuccessful actor, the struck-off doctor and so on; but there are prostitutes in the saloon – obvious ones – and it is implied that the landlord's wife, who isn't in fact his wife, has dabbled in the same profession. The barmaid, Ella, meanwhile, is entirely virtuous. She is well treated at the pub, but her mother wishes that she didn't work there, and a possible job as a governess is presented as a step up. Another escape route appears when she is courted by an older man, Mr Eccles, whose claim to eligibility is that he has 'a little something put by'. This money holds all the numinous gleam of the mirrored counter behind Ella's not-quite-pretty-enough head: she can scarcely bear the man, but knows she ought to marry him. Awful though he is, he is her 'chance'.

Ella is created with sad fondness, as a good, kind, sensible, unremarkable girl. She is Mr Eccles' superior in every salient way. Yet she is his supplicant: not just because she is poor, but because she is a barmaid. She does her work gamely – 'giving chaff for chaff' with the customers – but despite her innate dignity she feels a lurking social shame. She fears that she inhabits a world that is not respectable.

There is a sex complication here. A girl can't be too careful, and all that. Alongside Ella's story is that of Jenny – one of the prostitutes drinking in the Midnight Bell – who started life as a neat and exemplary servant and who, after one night of heavy drinking in a Hammersmith saloon, is set inexorably on the road to debasement. It is a morality tale, but it carries the weight of realism. To Jenny, pubs are 'haunts of destruction'. Given her story, she is quite right to see them this way, although the real agent of her downfall is her own extreme prettiness, which encourages her to dream in a way that her class does not permit. In a pub, however, she is exposed: spotlit as prey, and – after numerous large ports – entirely without her usual defences.

Ella, who does not have Jenny's allure, is less vulnerable

but also more out of place in the pub. And she is right to be anxious. A barmaid *did* have a tricky status, defended by her bar yet wholly exposed, negotiating a world of men with whom she is required to engage and pray to God every night that they behave. She has none of the power of the landlady; only the age-old female power, based upon biology and self-protection, to attract and deflect and – with luck – control the attentions of men.

But this is not only about femaleness. Ella's colleague, Bob, is a waiter in the saloon – some pubs enhanced the status of this bar with a smartly deferential table service – and he too finds himself struggling with the low status of his work, playing servant to prostitutes and to mean gits who toss him a derisive ha'penny as a tip. Neither Bob nor Ella is a snob. Both have a sense of tremulous self-worth. Yet both are vulnerable to the snobbery of others, to whom despite themselves they feel inferior, because of their association with a pub.

Patrick Hamilton is one of my favourite novelists, but when I first read him – by which time my grandmother had left her pub – I was pulled up somewhat by this viewpoint. Slightly troubled, if I am honest. Had I myself been judged because I was descended in the female line from publicans? It seemed both impossible and quite likely. It simply hadn't occurred to me that pubs, or my grandmother, might be seen as *declassée*. But then I didn't think much about class, in that personal sense, until university (where people seemed fairly obsessed with it). Before that, my engagement with the subject was merely abstract, something that I read about.

I read about the upper classes in Nancy Mitford, for instance, although it was only much later that I encountered this throwaway, in a letter to Evelyn Waugh, about the characters in Graham Greene's *The End of the Affair*: 'All that public house life, like poor people.' Nancy, bless her, wouldn't have known the first thing about pubs (for all her areas of worldliness, her idea of an everyday drinking establishment was probably White's). More interesting is Greene himself, who sort of *did* know. And I do remember, reading *Brighton Rock* when I was about thirteen, sensing a wrong note. When I reread the novel recently I sensed it again. Greene presents – quite brilliantly – a figure who could be seen as the very spirit of the pub, the landlady, the earthy magic that does not elevate but that miraculously lifts... Ida Arnold, with her friendly breasts and the taste of Guinness in her mouth, who spends afternoons in Brighton hotel rooms with weary, smiling, defeated men, who cocks her hat to an affirmative angle in the saloon mirror, who is defiantly non-respectable but believes in right and wrong: a fine figure of a woman, with no interest in saving souls and a determination to save Rose, a teenage waitress in love with the deadly boy gangster Pinkie. Ida takes life 'with a deadly seriousness'. Life is all. 'Life was sunlight on brass bedposts, Ruby port, the leap of her heart when the outsider you have backed passes the post and the colours go bobbing up.' The pub creed? Yes, one might say so. 'Be human,' says Ida, and to her it is as simple as that. That reality, for her, is enough; it is something worth having; it has to be, because for sure there is nothing else.

But Rose has a different creed, beyond the sunlit here and now. Like Pinkie she is a 'Roman', and believes in sin and damnation rather than wrongdoing and a hangman's rope. So she resists Ida's irreligious salvation with all the power that is in her, putting her faith in something inchoate yet profound.

I find Greene's highly charged Catholicism essentially silly; incredible, in both a literal and literary sense. I certainly don't believe it when Sarah renounces Bendrix for God in *The End of the Affair* (nor, incidentally, did Nancy Mitford, who said that the God she believed in liked people to be happy). I believe in Rose more, because she is so young. And *Brighton Rock* translates metaphor into action so dynamically that the struggle between Rose/Pinkie and Ida works, whether one believes in it or not. In the end it is a superb novel, therefore it carries its own power of conviction, which carries one along.

Nevertheless, there is this wrong note. Subjective, of course, but I hear contempt in Greene's description of Ida, and a rarefied snootiness in his portrayal of Rose and Pinkie. As George Orwell put it, Greene 'appears to share the idea... that there is something rather *distingué* about being damned'. Whereas Ida could not be less distinguished with her pieces of wisdom, arranged in her mind like cheap ornaments on a dresser, her hackneyed belief in law and order, her refusal to engage with anything more spiritual than a Ouija board. 'At one with the One – it didn't mean a thing beside a glass of Guinness on a sunny day.' How Greene judges her, beneath the veneer of understanding! 'She bore the same relation to passion as a peepshow.' Her hotel trysts are impure in a way that Pinkie's coupling with Rose is not; her easy willingness to have a drink with an old flame at eleven in the morning is set against Pinkie's fervid abstinence. Greene knows about Ida, he knows the world of the saloon, the casual pick-up, the sentimental songs, the tip for the 4.00 at Sandown, the good nature and the areas of indomitability. He knows it all, just as Patrick Hamilton does, but he holds it at arm's length.

If Ida Arnold embodies something like the spirit of the pub, the landlady, the chin up creed, then here, in *Brighton Rock*, is the intelligent case for the prosecution. 'Be human' is all very well. But it is not enough. It will not quite do as an everyday philosophy. There is a whole dimension beyond. And that may be so, but for all its subtlety, *Brighton Rock* does not convince me: I still sense the spectre of class, of a middle-class sensibility dazzled by the elitist rigours of Catholicism, and by its own ability to conjure the worldly bravura of an Ida.

As it happens she has a male counterpart, of sorts, in Patrick Hamilton's *The Slaves of Solitude*. He is a man in late middle age named Mr Prest, who lives at the Rosamund Tea Rooms boarding house but is not a boarding house type; he instead drinks every day in the local pubs and is 'regarded as being somehow beyond the pale'. Although the other residents do not know this, and think him a mere unplaceable nobody, Mr Prest is in fact a former music hall performer of some distinction. *Distingué*, even. This would not have enhanced his reputation in their eyes (Mr Thwaites would have considered Max Miller to be 'unnecessary'), but what they also do not know is that Mr Prest is politely uninterested in their opinion of him, and indeed regards the boarding house as 'a sort of zoo'.

The revelation whereby Mr Prest becomes the hero of *The Slaves of Solitude* is, to my mind, one of the most beautiful passages in twentieth-century literature. Like Ida Arnold, he can be seen as an embodiment of the spirit of the pub, of the 'be human' philosophy, but what is extraordinary is that in Patrick Hamilton's hands this *in itself* acquires another dimension: Mr Prest's very ordinariness and vulgarity has exactly that power. At the end of the novel he is given a part in a pantomime (a last-chance part, owing to the widespread wartime call-up of actors) and offers a ticket to his fellow resident Miss Roach, whom he likes, and who wants so much more from life than respectability can give her. Miss Roach watches from her stalls seat in a theatre in Wimbledon. There she sees, in a moment of simple blinding perception, that Mr Prest is 'going to be the hit of the show':

> The 'common' Mr Prest... Yes, indeed 'common' – very much 'commoner' here than at the Rosamund Tea Rooms – at moments vulgar perhaps – and yet, with these children, how very much the reverse of 'common', how shining, transfigured, and ennobled! ... Looking at him, she had a strong desire to cry...

And now, thinking of this passage, it mystifies me anew that Hamilton is often described as a cruel or cold novelist. There is such an intensity of compassion – such a touching authorial urgency – in the rendering of Mr Prest, who throughout much of the book remains shrouded within his beer-drinker persona, and whose values are so gloriously unveiled as the very obverse of those of the boarding house. Also of those of Rose and Pinkie, even though Mr Prest, apparently similar to Ida Arnold, is drawn from a very different standpoint. The self-regarding 'Romans' seem merely childish, wasteful of joy, with their pallid obsession with sin, in the face of Mr Prest, who deals in reality yet has 'the gift of public purification'. He imprints his giant personality upon the theatre and, in return, what earthy magic ensues and elevates!

Seen through the class prism, Mr Prest is common. But Patrick Hamilton, who understands perfectly the social structure as clung to by many of his characters, is offering another classification system, one that sweeps away tormenting anxieties such as those that beset Ella the barmaid. There are two basic categories of person in the England of Hamilton's novels: they are not placed above and below each other, but *en face*. They are, quite simply, the closed and the open class, or the mimsy and the robust class, or the narrow and the broad-minded class. Within those categories, any of the more familiar types can exist. In his novella *Unknown Assailant*, Hamilton portrays an aristocrat free of all snobbery and an ex-gamekeeper who thinks of nothing else. Then there is an Ella, naturally open of mind, trapped into pettiness by the limitations of those around her.

But it is in *The Slaves of Solitude*, set in wartime, that the undeclared war between the two classes is laid bare. The boarding house, which cringes old-maidishly from the tired, battered, adult, pugilistic-looking Mr Prest, has no idea that what it disapproves of is:

> the very backbone of his culture: that his own upbringing and manner of life, his music-hall history, his achievements, his traditions, his friends, the fact that he had been associated with and could still call by their Christian names many well-known stars both of the past and present, speaking, if he went to town, their liberal and racy language in public houses... that all these things were to Mr Prest reasons, not for faint opprobrium, but for complacence and pride.

On certain happy days Mr Prest leaves the town where he is presently unhappily housed, and goes to the West End, there to fall into felicitous company and spend the day with his old London acquaintance. He returns 'full of drink, certainly, but fuller still of the day behind him... of the humour, humanity, spaciousness and grandeur of that manner of life'.

And there, if you like, is the spirit of the pub. Not every pub; not everything about the pub: just the pub.

My grandmother was nothing like Mr Prest, but she belonged to the same category of person. In a way that now seems to me very important, if life is to be valued, the pair of them represent the same thing. When I was growing up, wonderfully ignorant of the class system that might view a landlady as being 'not quite nice', I was nevertheless aware of my grandmother as a member of the robust class, the kind who poured spirits into a decanter then glugged the surplus from the bottle, as against people who were of the opposite class: certain of my friends' parents, for instance, whom I now recognise as the kind of people who might write to the newspapers regarding a change to the broadcast time of *The Archers*.

People of this kind – some of whom were extremely nice, as well as 'nice' – might have thought that a landlady was a *declassée* profession, but the fact is that when any of them met my grandmother, they collapsed beneath the insouciant weight of her personality. Looking back, I can think of nobody who was not impressed by her. They may have got her wrong – seen her as a 'character'; believed her to be an Ida, which she most definitely was not – but they always responded to her, to that old-style breadth of being. She was not just a landlady, after all. She was the supreme landlady, with all that was best in the breed writ large upon her. And in the usual English sense of the word 'class', she was simply impossible to categorise. Unlike Mr Prest she never looked common, even in her most flagrant leopard-print/ankle-chain ensembles, while her speech was a mixture of posh locutions ('weskit' for waistcoat, 'gorn' and 'sod orf') and the frankly demotic ('Goodbye, Mrs Big Tits!' she would mouth from the window, waving at a well-upholstered customer waddling off to a car with Playtex-ed zeppelins aloft).

She was classless, in fact. Through and through. Nothing to do with class bothered her. She was as indifferent to its niceties as it is possible to be, just as she was to those of political affiliation, race, sexuality, all the things that now fill us with such tremulous angst. If a person was the right sort – which meant the large-spirited sort, 'liberal and racy' – then that was what mattered, over and above anything else: better a dustman who fought to buy his round than a duke who slithered out of doing so. (One must be honest here, a duke who bought his round would have been even more welcome.)

Of course not everybody in her pub was that type of person. Some were mimsy but kind, so it didn't matter. Some were downright small-minded, not in the way that precluded going to pubs but in other, nastier ways. That too had to be accepted. Nevertheless, one of my grandmother's finer moments came when a young black man came into the pub with his white girlfriend – an unusual sight at that time, in that rural location – and not-quite-inaudible mutterings emerged from a couple of the less attractive regulars. They were good customers, but she wasn't having it. She bustled them into the courtyard outside the pub and went coldly berserk. I also recall a gay friend of mine, meeting her with his partner when she was in her nineties, and saying to me afterwards how wonderful she had been; I could see that he had feared that an old country woman, which ostensibly she then was, might be prejudiced against homosexuality. I didn't tell him about Lot and Lil, the gay couple who had drunk at her father's pub, to whom she had lent her black velvet evening gowns for parties. During the war (probably around the same time the forces of law caught Ivor Novello for 'petrol coupon fraud') one of the parties was raided, the men were arrested – wearing the black velvet – and doubtless jailed.

'I never got the dresses back, no.' She had lived through that era; she lived on into the age of virtue-signalling, and throughout it all she remained unchanged. This was part of her genius.

She was a pragmatist, not a paragon. There was nothing politicised about her liberalism (indeed politics was another subject to which she showed a professional indifference; other than when people 'had a bit of a moan', it was off limits in the pub). Although what she hated more than anything was meanness of any kind, her generosity somehow went alongside her self-absorption; it had a dispassionate quality. It was essential to her landlady's gift but it was also innate, more like an instinct than a choice.

She was a natural bohemian, really. Her soul was forged in a world that for better or worse no longer exists, that centred upon London. My grandmother left the city as a young girl in the early 1930s, when her father took on the licence of the old pub, situated in a Home Counties town some twenty miles away. I suppose London pubs were hard to come by. But they were always London people, and they brought that to their pub. My great-grandmother would sit by the window in her new home and watch the Green Line bus on its road to smoggy paradise. My grandmother also remained a London person. I remember one of her last outings, a visit to the Royal Opera House for her birthday; how she had stared silently out of the car window at the Mall, the Strand, the dirty gold streetlights dancing on the dusk.

From the early days of the pub that I knew, which by the time the brewery had done its work looked the very ideal of the country establishment, she would take a day off every week and go to London. These days, these sacred Tuesdays, she spoke of later with something almost like emotion. Sometimes she drove herself, chain-smoking Passing Clouds as she negotiated West End streets that would now seem shockingly empty, devoid of signage and regulation, on her way to shop for all the things that her new life lacked: clothes in satin and taffeta, perky little hats, food with a taste of the foreign, scent of a richness to pierce and fill the country air, lipstick to brighten the dim saloon, sleek and blackened hair. All this meant either Knightsbridge – green and gold bags, Mr Teasy-Weasy – or the austere opulence of Bond Street, where she would park for an entire afternoon without fear of penalty. These were female outings, with a girlfriend and later my mother. On the way home, always on 'A' roads (the motorway being one of the few things that alarmed her), she would stop at the Sea Shell on Lisson Grove to buy fish and chips.

But the more truly precious occasions involved Victor; not so much for the man himself as for the possibilities that only came, in those days, with male accompaniment. Victor meant the shows, the first night of *My Fair Lady*, cabaret at the Talk of the Town – where the mirrored interior reflected an infinity of red mouths and bare shoulders, where Pearl Bailey beckoned Princess Margaret from the audience to be the foil in her sublime act – and the Palladium stars who scattered charisma like fairy dust. Sometimes these West End evenings were shared with another couple, pub customers, who were of apparently similar type: sophisticates without cynicism. My grandmother and Victor would dine with this pair at the Caprice, until the friendship became a bore, and for a curious reason.

A particular table was used by Princess Margaret (her again). The couple regarded it as a point of honour to eat at this table, and would wait it out for long ravenous minutes at the bar until it became free. My grandmother and Victor were not like that. They had nothing of the mindset that worships celebrity and seeks a kind of osmosis with it. They had too much humour, too much self-assurance; 'always thought I was as good as anybody else' was one of my grandmother's shrugged phrases. So they gradually extricated themselves from ties to the Caprice couple. Generally, I think, they were happier à deux. Not because they longed to gaze into each other's eyes, but because they sought and found the same things in London. Their experience was shared, not in the sense that it co-mingled, but because it was so similar for both of them.

Soho, for instance, where to walk the streets was to traverse the blatant, secretive, gleaming bars of an outdoor pub, whose ceiling was the blue-black sky. Victor was 'known' in Soho. He flourished, became a relaxed and worldly man rather than my grandmother's faintly de trop courtier, moved easily from place to place with a memory of glory still swirling around him. The musicians in Denmark Street offered him their hands; he had been one of them, had played guitar with 'Lewis', whom on one occasion he took my grandmother to meet backstage (she remembered Armstrong as dignified, remote, one hand busily staunching a lip that bled from his exertions). Then there was Berwick Street Market; the French House pub that my grandmother always called by its original name, the York Minster; Wheeler's on Old Compton Street; Isow's on Brewer Street... all of this was what my grandmother brought back to the pub, trailing the hallowed vestiges of London: of sharp, wry shouts; doorways glowing dirty red; quickly dispensed drinks slid with neat aplomb onto tired wooden counters; tables shaded and angled with intimacy; the sense of the unpredictable, the infinite, the impossibly energetic; of life played out amid the floodlights; of the Windmill Theatre and its inexorable winking reminder that it never closed; of a night that was ephemeral yet carved in some dimension of time upon the dark air...

These evenings could not have existed without alcohol. That was not, however, the point of them. Victor was a man of moderate appetites (except for cigarettes), one of those naturally spry and trim-waisted Londoners; also he had his Daimler waiting faithfully on Lexington Street. Driving wouldn't have prevented him drinking, but he wouldn't have overdone it. And my grandmother had a business to run the next day. Sometimes she and Victor would call time after Wheeler's, from which they took lovingly parcelled-up cartons of mussel soup (in later years this would be inflicted upon my parents, holding the fort at the pub and dreading the soup). Sometimes they would have a row, which cut the evening short: on one occasion Victor threw a tantrum when a waiter did his 'more black pepper, madam?' routine with too much feeling. For all the easy habitude of their relationship, its terms were essentially dictated by my grandmother, and from time to time this ripped through the cloak of Victor's urbanity.

Sometimes, however, they would decide that the night was still young. My grandmother *was* young, by today's standards – not yet forty – although a photograph of her dancing at a Licensed Victuallers' ball shows a definitely mature woman, with an unabashed adult glamour that no longer really exists. She looks like Gwyneth Paltrow's mother, figuratively speaking, but she also looks sexy in a deep, lived, knowing, fearless way.

Despite her bond with the pub, she resented the idea of returning when it might still be open. Indeed, if that happened she would sit in the car and wait until everybody had gone. So she did usually move on to a club, occasionally the Colony Room, where again Victor was 'known'. This powerfully atmospheric hole on Dean Street was of course much favoured by artists (and hangers-on), among them Lucian Freud and Francis Bacon. According to my grandmother's legend, she once observed Bacon scrawling a drawing on a napkin, or a tablecloth, or a bit of paper, I was never sure about the details, which was then left lying around; she could have picked it up with the greatest of ease, surrounded as she was by semi-catatonics, but she did not do so. Nor, it seemed, did she regret the omission. 'Oh, well he was such a terrible drunk.' This was one of her familiar contradictions: the reverence for alcohol and the loathing of drunkards. 'Falling over – you know, deliberate-like.'

In fact the Colony was not really her milieu. She would have coped with it, and liked the idea of it (the club was still relatively new at that time, having opened in 1948, so it had not had the chance to become a parody of itself). But she enjoyed the push-pull of subverted decorum more than the 'evening cunty, who's *she* been fucking today' idiom, which anyway wasn't shocking because there was nobody shockable present. She perceived the conscious theatricality of a Bacon, playing to a gallery that knew pretty much exactly what to expect. Again that wasn't her style. Her own play-acting was merely a heightened version of herself, done not to impress but because it came naturally. Putting on a full-blown act was almost always done with the aim of impressing, as often as not by people who had no need to impress. Nerves, she would have said.

Still, the Colony was *something*. My grandmother was not indifferent to the stature of Francis Bacon and, although she never claimed to know her, she would have respected (not feared) the club's presiding presence, Muriel Belcher, who ran the place for thirty years. She would have known what it took to be a Muriel, that daily effort made by the true hostess, who gave of herself without stint (even when being vile, caustic, vicious, terrifying – it was all part of the show). 'Hostesse' is a medieval word for what we would today call a landlady – Mistress Quickly is described as a hostess – although with the development of pubs the two terms split into slightly different meanings. But with a landlady such as my grandmother, a large personality in a small and club-like establishment, there was scarcely any difference at all.

So would she have done better – I now wonder – to have been a hostess proper, in charge of her own London club? Was she, indeed, circumscribed by class in the conventional sense of the word, by the fact that her father had to work his way up to the status of landlord, and that acquiring his own establishment represented the ultimate in achievement, that he was a man with every advantage of personality and none of birth? However suited my grandmother was to the trade that she inherited, had there ever been much choice about it? Except marriage, of course: a man like her suitor Nat Tennens, owner of the Kilburn Empire, represented the real choice in those days, but she had had no desire to take it.

I can see her, yes, in the dark glow of a Soho club, accepting the ironic homage of the members. I can't see her encouraging their more hysterical excesses. She disliked the lack of control that spilled over into anarchy and, for all her bohemianism, she was deeply respectable. She preferred the taut flirtation across the saloon counter to the frank exchanges of the Brighton hotel room. The more sordid connotations of the word 'hostess' would have appalled her. But there were different kinds of clubs, just as there were pubs; they did not have to be drunken or disreputable. She could have run somewhere plusher, more Mayfair, more *salon*-like, and I am sure that she would have done it wonderfully well.

Nevertheless, there is something not quite right about the image of this parallel universe. For a start my grandmother herself loved pubs. If she entered a good pub, she inhaled and expanded, emanating not exactly pleasure but the animal sense of being restored to her rightful habitat. There were things that the pub lacked, most assuredly, of the cosmopolitan and the chic. It could be rich in tedium and terrible conversations ('How are you tonight; not three bad'), its customers could try the patience of a far saintlier woman than my grandmother ('Well they're not the ticket, are they, some of them'). But it was precisely this humbleness, this street-corner accessibility, that gave the pub something that the club did not have. Pubs were loved, in a way that is not quite possible with clubs. With its innate selectivity the club creates a self-conscious *hauteur*, a sense of belonging quite different to that of the mongrel pub, where everybody is allowed to belong, unless informed otherwise. Nor does the club camaraderie generate much warmth, but perhaps warmth is a provincial thing to expect from a night out... That extraordinary play by Rodney Ackland, *Absolute Hell*, has it about right. It is set in 1945, in a Soho establishment run by a boozed-up hostess who includes among her regulars a failing writer, a lesbian literary critic, a film producer with an ill-treated acolyte, a good-time girl, a GI out for a good time: the usual suspects, in fact, but the play goes deep beneath cliché. It reeks of spirituous atmosphere, it is Hamiltonian in its feel for the rhythms of drunkenness ('I'm going off the boil,' somebody says, meaning, 'For Christ's sake, top me up'), and it understands how the club becomes a willingly entered prison to the people who need it. None more so than the hostess, Christine, who gives her all to the place and gets remarkably little in return, perhaps because there is interdependency but not much kindness. People talk as they do in Chekhov, in a vacuum. They parade their vulnerabilities like desperate party pieces, as a way of singing for their liquid supper, although the offer of a large whisky is as much as anything a means to get them to shut up. They want love – impersonal love as much as the other sort – and there is not much of it to be found.

Would a good pub be as devoid of consolation? I think not. Of course the general behaviour is very much as above: putting on a front, getting a round in when the mood threatens to darken, having a laugh; that, after all, is the point of going out (or used to be). One is not on a visit to a shrink or to one's mother.

And yet, in a good pub, empathy is always implied. I am thinking of the sad trio on the settle in my grandmother's public bar, towards whom people were brisk and cheerful and, without really doing anything, kind. It was the kindness that came with a lack of self-importance, with a constant awareness of there but for the grace of God... On occasion I would see my grandmother in some corner of the saloon, talking to one or other of the customers with an intensity of empathy – privately, albeit in public. Later – when I was old enough to divine the reality within these images – I realised that they had been talking about the things that lay beneath the smiling veneer: the breakdown of a marriage, the lump in a breast, the unrequited love for some man or other, the fear that a wife was playing around. Drink made confession easier, but so did the embracing chamber of the pub. So too did the disinterested flavour of my grandmother's kindness, which was nonetheless absolute.

My grandmother thought a lot of herself, she knew that she was awash with personality, but she never thought herself too good for the pub. She too had the gift of ordinariness.

Although she liked what she called 'swank', she had a sort of divine good sense, an earthbound quality that suited her so completely to the landlady life. It was bred in her, no doubt. It was the aspect that enabled her to cut to the heart of motive, and preside over the kitchen conversations with such omniscience. She could have chatted with just the same assurance about the people she encountered in a club like the Colony: 'Well, he reckons there's a few quid there, doesn't he,' or, 'He wasn't half showing orf to that young girl, I suppose he thought he was in,' or, 'They think they can drink, my old farmers would drink them under the table.' This last was probably true. Some years later I took a boyfriend to the pub, a man who in London circles was regarded as a bit of a dasher, and we fell into an evening with the farmers, men who in their amiable way ate him for breakfast. He tried to fence with them, which was hopeless; he tried to drink with them, which was calamitous. As he sulked and swayed, so they remained alert, good-humoured, ready for more, and despite myself I couldn't help but think the worse of the boyfriend.

Something else about my grandmother: she liked to be in charge. From the age of fifteen she had presided from behind the bar. She was *dauphine*, queen, priestess, on the whole the most interesting person around. In a club or (if Victor had had his way) a hotel, the balance of power is slightly different: she would have been up against the customers' personalities, a situation that might not have been quite to her taste. In the pub she was within herself. At home.

I remember now another of her stories, told as usual as if I already knew it, about a pub a few streets away from her father's, of similar stamp but less successful. The daughter of this pub's landlord was a few years older than my grandmother, equally attractive although in pure English style. In youth she too served behind the bar and received the adoration owing to the *dauphine*; this, however, was not enough for her. She went to London, became a C. B. Cochran chorus girl, went to Hollywood, married one of the biggest film stars of the day and ended up the wife of an earl.

This landlord's daughter was a pre-feminism feminist who used her femaleness as decorated armoury and believed that fate could be forged rather than accepted. Which sounds very much like my grandmother, who was no less bold and glamorous, no less dynamic; yet her attitude to fate was slightly different. In the mid-1930s, when she was about eighteen, a pub customer who worked in cinema invited her to spend the next couple of weeks filming at Elstree; an extras job only, but it was the sort of chance that the other landlord's daughter would have grasped and shaped to her own ends. My grandmother got up at five, did one day on set then never went back. She simply didn't want it. In later life she often talked about the girl around the corner who became a countess, and did so without a shred of envy; she was honestly, contentedly, merely intrigued by the progress of her parallel self.

The ordinariness of the pub, which is so integral, makes it singularly resonant as a setting for the extraordinary. Watson and Crick, announcing the discovery of the secret of life to the lunchtime drinkers at the Eagle in Cambridge. Lewis and Tolkien, ruminating on fantasy worlds in the parlour-like spaces of the Eagle and Child in Oxford. Ron Kray raising the gun to George Cornell as the drinkers at the Blind Beggar stared resolutely into their pint glasses. Lady Lucan running into the Plumbers' Arms in Belgravia, barefoot and head clotted with blood, screaming at the sparse assemblage that her nanny had been killed. Ruth Ellis glimpsed through the window of the Magdala in Hampstead, where the Easter Monday drinkers would soon hear the sound of gunfire in the street outside.

Ruth Ellis shot her lover, who had treated her abysmally. Today she would almost certainly have been tried for manslaughter. Sixty years ago she was convicted of murder and became the last woman to be hanged. The man who executed her, Albert Pierrepoint, had another trade: he ran a pub in Oldham called Help the Poor Struggler, acquired with the proceeds from despatching Nazi war criminals. By all accounts he was a good publican, full of bonhomie. But imagine the deployment of power by such a landlord (people knew who he was, although he did not discuss it), a man who in his secondary career executed more than 400 people, pulling pints with his deft hangman's hands; let us just say that any masochistic tendency within his customers would have been peculiarly stimulated.

Not that public opinion – therefore pub opinion – was necessarily against what Pierrepoint did. For instance there was little sympathy for Ruth Ellis, my grandmother told me, shaking her head in a characteristic mixture of dismay and forbearance. The trial had taken place in the summer of 1955, when the pub was truly hitting its stride, filled with bands of airy sunlight through which the dust motes glinted and danced, with short-sleeved customers who over-spilled to the outside tables, forming little concentrations of warmth and delight. Ruth Ellis was discussed, naturally, by most of these carefree drinkers. She had run a club, one of the loucher type, and her rouged and varnished demeanour – which she maintained, hostess-style, at the Old Bailey – hid her vulnerability from view. It was as if she herself had wanted it that way. She had her standards. She didn't try to incite pity for the miscarriage that her lover had brought on with a punch to the stomach, she didn't rat on whoever had given her the gun. It was about pride, in a man's world. But the attitude to Ruth Ellis exposed the fragility of status for women in her kind of job. 'They all thought she was a tart, you see,' my grandmother explained. Which she had been, in a manner of speaking; although she might have been labelled one, whatever the truth of the matter; take a woman away from the *mise en scène* of the bar, and the adulation of men could turn at speed into condemnation.

My grandmother's own attitude, I sensed, had been one of solidarity, warily expressed. There could be no outright identification of herself with the wretched Mrs Ellis (which, oddly enough, was her own name); that was not the landlady's job. But she would have paid glancing tribute to both the woman ('poor bugger') and her adherence to the 'chin up' philosophy ('she's got some pluck'). She would have behaved in the same way at her own trial, had she been in that position, which she would not have been.

Conversely, she remembered sympathy for a local man who killed and dismembered his wife during the war. This was not entirely about gender. In part it was simply because the man was known to people. Also the crime had almost certainly been committed without premeditation. Despite the dismemberment, which was attributed to panic, this man was regarded with a measure of compassion – more so than the apparently ruthless Ruth, who admitted the intent to kill; but also far more than the wife-murderer at my grandmother's pub, who would later plead provocation with such remarkable success. Of course in the 1940s the shadow of that cheery Lancashire publican, Pierrepoint, loomed over the local murderer. A petition was placed on the counter and, as my grandmother recalled, most customers were falling over themselves to sign it; the death sentence was indeed commuted, although these reprieves seem to have been more a matter of luck than anything else.

This was at the old pub, in the town-dark public bar, where men screwed a Player's Weight into their mouths and said go on then, pass us a pen, I'll sign for the poor bastard. There but for the grace of God.

The old pub is now renamed, rebuilt, its former incarnation completely forgotten except for what I am about to write, which comes only through the memories of my grandmother. As ever, she seemed unaware that she was telling me things I could not possibly know. This was history, folklore, the template: to know any proper pub was to know the old pub.

I had realised that, surely?

It was true, that my grandmother's pub contained the soul of this other unknown pub along with its shiny black settles, its brass fire tools with their honey gleam, its Royal Albert and squat decanters and a handful of its photographs, which held the occluded gleam of memory itself. In externals the two establishments could scarcely have been less alike, although in essence this meant little. But whereas my grandmother's pub was the perfect specimen of the rural inn, so the old pub was supremely of the streets, with its stern dark wood and dull gold fittings, its inn sign of black glass and gilded calligraphy, its swing doors with their quick yielding creak and flap of air, its windows etched with ghostly writing – SALOON, FINE ALES – and its interior light, striped with the yellow glare of street lamps, sharply shadowed, briskly mysterious.

It was an enormous place, fronting on to one street and backing on to another. Beside it was the church, and every which way there were shops: a grocer, a cobbler, a butcher, all run by and filled with pub customers. When my great-grandfather took it over in the 1930s it was fairly new, built after the first war (to which a couple of my great-uncles absconded, adding to their ages as boys then did, and for a wonder surviving). During the war, dreams of relative temperance had flowered again: the 1914 Defence of the Realm act restricted opening hours to five and a half each day, and beer was proudly diluted. Two years later, pubs in three disparate areas – Carlisle, Cromarty and Enfield – were taken into state management (a few remained so until

1973). They had no incentive to sell alcohol, as there was no profit to be made on it, and food became a central feature; the idea being that the wholesome pie or turnip bread or roasted marrowbones would mitigate the demon drink. This was very much like the Refreshment Association quasi-pub conceived by Bernard Shaw.

The desire to make pubs about eating, rather than drinking, was a policy urged by the temperance movement in the early twentieth century – by which time it would have realised that outright prohibition was never going to happen – and the war made it a great deal easier to foist upon people. I now realise that this was why my great-grandfather so vehemently opposed food in pubs. He was Chestertonian in his belief that the state was a bloody nuisance (my grandmother took a similar view) and that the pub was a place where one could thankfully ignore its nonsense, while incidentally doing some of its job. The idea that drinkers should be forced to eat – with the authorities acting like an almighty dinner lady, pushing pies into the mouths of people who simply wanted their pint – would have outraged him. 'A pub's a pub, not a bloody *cayff*' (he meant café). Food in his establishment consisted of arrowroot biscuits and Smith's crisps – plain only – kept in a tub on the counter with a screw-top lid. People sprinkled their crisps with the little bag of salt inside the packet, then threw a couple of grains over their left shoulder 'into the face of the devil'. My grandmother did this all her life.

She also maintained her father's suspicion of food. Cheddar and Ritz crackers, gherkins and olives, crisps and peanuts – these were not *food*, they were merely punctuation within the smooth paragraphs of drink. Later, at her own establishment, she treasured the remark of one of the courteous, remote men who would descend periodically from the brewery to cast a cool eye upon their showpiece; he inhaled as he entered and said: 'How nice to come into a pub and not smell food.' He preferred the adult essence of beer and fug. Today this would seem perverse in the extreme, but not so, not so long ago.

This man from the brewery was endorsing my great-grandfather, in fact, and that pleased my grandmother because she had worshipped him. However much she loved her sweet-natured homely mother, it was her father whom she 'studied' (as she put it) and sought to become. There was something almost mythic in her sense of herself as the Publican's Daughter. It was strange, really; she had five older brothers, all of whom worked at the pub before marrying and moving on, but felt that it was she who should carry on the tradition. She believed that she had the strongest calling. She also had the old-fashioned daughter's sense that she should not leave her parents, not that she wanted to.

So when she married, not long before the outbreak of the second war, she clearly thought that she was acquiring a future co-publican as well as a husband. Had she not divorced, she would of course have automatically inherited the old pub's licence, although my grandfather may have had other ideas. She once told me a story of how, during the brief span of her marriage – spent in the pub's enormous upstairs quarters; the imminence of war meant that they never even started to find a home – the family had been having tea together and suddenly her husband had upended the whole table, cups and cake and all. She was a little stirred by the memory; also amused and comprehending. 'Well, he was fed up, you know. With me, I suppose.' She knew that she had been a poor proposition as a wife. She had fallen in love, married, had a baby, but had wanted nothing else to change. She had believed that my grandfather would slot obediently into the pub, and he had had a moment of frustrated youthful rebellion against the whole pint-pulling lot of them. I understood it too. Both him and her. Mainly her. I have never been the marrying kind, although once or twice I thought that I should try to be; when she told me this story – elliptically, vividly – I felt as close to her as it was possible to get.

And what would have happened, had the war not intervened and saved my grandmother from making a decision – the pub or the man – I really cannot imagine. But after her husband joined up, tacitly ending the relationship, she seems to have decided never to be susceptible again. Perhaps, having watched from behind the bar the idiocies and shenanigans caused by passion, she deliberately called time on romantic love. Not on men, whom she always adored, but in the idea of a man as the point of everything, a solution to life.

No: the man whom she most valued was always her father, the charismatic little charmer crackling with wry vitality. She talked about him constantly, in that litany-like way of hers: repetitive but never boring, because enigmatic. He died many years before I was born and I know little of him, except a handful of his sayings, such as the toast to wives and sweethearts, may they never meet; or no place like home, when you've got nowhere else to go; or (at the prospect of something unpleasant) I'd rather sleep with a dead policeman. I know what he looked like, from the photograph that hung in my grandmother's sitting room: kindly of eye, immaculate of collar, cigar held steady in his mouth, Jewish ancestry nobly apparent. The image was so familiar to me that I held the imprint of its faded black and white on my mind's eye, although I had never *thought* about it. Now I think, as I do about all true publicans, what a force he must have had: the young Paddington 'cellarman' of the 1901 census, born soon after the legislation that finally created the pub, who rose to become the architect of a proper house, a house with a name, a beloved house, the spirit of what that law was all about. I know what he must have been like, because of how much my grandmother emulated him.

Also among her small collection was a photograph of the old pub itself. It was a close-up of the bar, nothing more – in Hulton Getty tones, not quite sepia, more a sombre maroon-brown – but it thrilled me as a Sickert would have done. So rich in recessive depths, within which lay something so meaningfully, so meaninglessly, ordinary: just the world as it was when the pub was so intrinsic as to be scarcely noticeable, simply the screensaver to one's life. How I craved entry to that photograph, for one evening! To smell the wax polish on the wood, the overflow of beer beneath the pumps, the nostril-burning cigarettes – and to be unaware of it all, to *be*. Behind the bar stood a couple of my grandmother's female cousins, snoods on their hair, capable arms, smiles fixed momentarily for the camera but otherwise without self-consciousness. They had no image of themselves. Nor did the man caught in the corner of the photo, leaning on the bar with his shoulders slightly humped and hat brim low, hands cradling a glass. It was the age-old stance of the pub customer, seeking an oblique comfort. To me it looked configurative, symbolic, all the more so because eighty years ago the man himself was just standing there.

Beyond that tableau, what did the old pub look like? I can only piece it together: the image is incomplete, a sensory muddle of businesslike jostle and sponged suits and snoods and dark tints and low jovial shouts plaiting the thickened air. I realise now that it seems to me *pub-like* in a way that my grandmother replicated but could never achieve so unthinkingly, because the old pub belonged to a world so at one with it.

I realise, too, that I have never actually been in a pub like this must have been. A huge town place, with unusually long bars, the public and saloon joined together in an extended oval that was separated by the counter. A veritable chorus line could have stood behind that counter, working the multiplicity of pumps, keeping the beer engine stoked and revved. In shape it was not unlike the Midnight Bell off the Euston Road, which was created by Patrick Hamilton in 1929, not long before the time I am describing, and whose saloon was 'narrow and about thirty feet in length'. How could such a place exist today? How could a room that size be kept alive, quite naturally, without the false hilarity of extreme drunkenness? Yet this one was. Footsteps turned constantly towards the old pub, just as they did the nearby dog track, or the large Victorian theatre (later a bingo hall, later still derelict) where Gracie Fields and Todd Slaughter went to give their respective shows, Sally from the Alley and Sweeney Todd the Demon Barber.

This was life in the mid-1930s, communal pleasure as defiance against economic depression, the threat of war; and in the midst of it all my great-grandfather, an ageing man by then, but doing his bit to cheer the civilian troops. I believed my grandmother when she told me about his popularity, his straightforward standing within the community. It is only now that I wonder about that surname, Solomon, in the context of the times (Mosley was already on the march when the family left London). One of my great-uncles was uncomfortably aware of it. But my grandmother – and by implication her father – were far too confident to care; she knew all about anti-Semitism, as indeed how could one not in the 1930s, but she would have disdained it with the same breezy, oddly piercing contempt that she did all expressions of petty-mindedness. As a person who liked most things about herself, she very much liked her Jewish blood (which was on one side only; her mother had none). Although without religion, she gravitated to Isow's restaurant and Grodzinski's of Golders Green with something like instinct – which sounds outlandishly shallow, yet was not. At the very end of her life she had her father's face, the ancient Semitic lines emerging as the female trappings fell away.

Sometimes her memory unfurled for me with ease. What

the men drank in the public bar, where they stood on the tiled floor and sat at workmanlike square tables: Black and Tan, Brown and Mild, Light and Bitter, Double Diamond, Mackeson. What the women drank in the carpeted saloon, from within the firm luxury of the green leather bucket chairs: Gin and Orange, Gin and Pep, Gin and Lime, Port and Lemon, Egg Flips, Green Goddess. What people smoked: Craven A, Passing Cloud, Du Maurier, Chesterfield, Woodbine, Albany, Black Cat, Capstan, de Reszkes, Player's Navy Cut, Player's Weights, Player's Perfecto (so desirable and smart that they could be bought singly from vending machines). The games the customers played: darts, shove ha'penny, dominoes, bar billiards (for a shilling a time). On occasion, a small band of 'novelty' darts players would turn up, like an intimate music hall act, and throw treble 20s with long nails or screws. Yes... and did people play cards, I asked her, like you did – solo, brag? No, she said, because you couldn't play for money. Nothing for money, not for years (1961, in fact, was when the law on gambling changed). Like you couldn't have a bet on the gees, which everybody wanted to do – well, you know that. Yes, I did know that. No off-course betting until the first bookmakers opened, 1961 again... but of course, my grandmother said, it went on. I mean old Woodbine Minnie, the bookie's runner, she'd come shuffling round taking the bets...

Woodbine Minnie in her hat and hairnet was one of the very few women who entered the public bar, where the drinks were cheaper and beer was served in a straight glass. In the saloon it came in a tankard. This distinction still existed at my grandmother's pub, although by that time there was no class element. Tankards were the norm but there would always be somebody who would insist severely on a *straight glass*, as if a tankard might contain some residual poison, just as there were those who wanted gin in a small bowl glass and others who could drink it only from a tumbler – it was a means whereby which the customers asserted themselves. As for those who had 'special' tankards, including one man whose tankard was so special that its silver handle was in the form of a naked woman... they were another category altogether, the kind that my grandmother referred to as 'proper soppy'.

And then, she told me, there were the other bars in the old pub, the secretive ones that stood at either end of the long main room and were entered by the back street. One was the jug and bottle. This had a hatch, opening on to the counter and screened by a row of opaque 'windows' suspended above the bar at eye level, so that faces were obscured. When the customer wanted a drink they would twist one of the windows and hiss the order into the gap. Discretion was all, in the jug and bottle. Women, often elderly widows or spinsters and therefore unable – in their own view – to drink inside a pub, would come with their own receptacle and have it filled with beer. Before they walked home, clutching their takeaway, they might sit in the tiny bar with its delicious fire, and have their palms read by my great-grandmother. She didn't particularly know what she was doing; it was just a kindness. Like my own mother she was not a pub person. Her domain was the living quarters, the two floors upstairs with their giant, incongruous spaces: a ballroom with splendid windows overlooking the road, a sitting room with a balcony above the huge backyard, where she would serve tureens of steaming stew to local tramps (the pub as sanctuary again). There is a photograph of that yard, dating from when the family first moved to the pub and were assembled for the camera. A good-looking bunch, on the whole, although there was a mysterious stony-faced cousin with the aspect of an escaped criminal (one of the unmarried Adas or Ivys who was always staying at the pub. They lent a hand but the favour was really to them; 'surplus women' did not have an easy time of it). My great-grandmother, clutching a marvellous roguish dog, had a face of mellow curves in which I could divine a faint look of my grandmother. *She*, meanwhile, doll-like beneath her cloud of black hair, had an aspect that I had never thought to see in her: she looked childish. At that point, she was still the girl who had truanted from her convent. I have no idea what she dreamed of doing with her life at that point.

She was enrolled in the high school, but there is no education like growing up in a pub. For instance, there was the interesting truth about the other back bar, at the opposite end to the jug and bottle. On Friday evenings a uniformed copper would make an entrance at the pub, striding through in his clattering boots and tall helmet, no doubt getting a kick out of the change in atmosphere – from merry to wary – that he instantly created. This done, he would sidle off and drink the pint that was waiting for him in the private cupboard-like bar, known as 'the policeman's'.

The fact that an officer of the law had a craving for a little of what the pub offered, the fact that he could be a hypocrite, putting the fear of God into everybody while dreaming of his foaming tankard – this was the sort of thing that my grandmother saw. She also saw the pub tarts: Queenie, the plain little woman who sat demure and immobile in the saloon – 'I couldn't understand it, you know. Nice-looking men, some of them, and they'd go orf with her' – and Nell, starched and upright as a Sunday schoolmistress. She saw the pub villain, Kingston Jack, who deployed wiles and winks and got friendly with would-be shrewd saps like the butcher, who, as it happened, had some savings to invest... 'He turned him over, oh yes.' She saw the man whose older sister was revealed to be his mother, and the ripples of intrigued compassion that formed around him as this truth disseminated itself, pub-style. She saw the division between the public and the saloon bars, so eloquent of the English class system that pubs could otherwise obliterate. She saw the discreet illicit movements beneath the round saloon tables, the adulterous interlinking of hands, the tentative nudge of a stockinged ankle. She saw the bob and weave of the men as they boasted and shoved each other, teased and played power games with each other, bristled and squared up to each other, smiled and tolerated each other, and when the evening had reached a certain pitch fairly loved each other. She saw Lot and Lil, the gay couple; the actors who came in from the theatre, including the very young Richard Attenborough; the theatre manager, who would later turn up with his friend Nat Tennens, my grandmother's most eligible suitor; the dog men from the nearby greyhound track, with their rueful losers' shrugs; the men who had suffered from the dire diseases of that time – polio, TB – and were left halt or frail, with dragging legs or caved-in chests, but who still turned up and counted out their pennies for a pint; the boxers whose fights were staged at a nearby venue, one of whom would fall beneath her lush spell; the bay rum-scented factory owners in their bespoke suits and finely tilted hats... she saw it all, the same scenes that I saw but painted in deeper, sootier shades, and she was shrewder about it than I. Although I have a reverence for female wisdom, I do not innately possess it; she, perforce, did. I saw it all through a kind of haze, but she picked out the patterns with the confidence of a code-breaker.

Of course I had another life. For her the pub was life, the all and only.

When she first arrived at the old pub, she was not officially 'out'. She wheeled a pram through cobbled streets to the local tannery, collecting the block of ice from which pieces would be chipped and put into drinks. She carried a great bag of coppers, £5 worth and 'sodding heavy', to be exchanged at the local bus station. She helped to pack crates for the draymen, who still came with their magnificent horses. She took a regular jug of mild to an old lady who was unable to walk the half-mile to the pub, and who would present her on arrival with a steaming baked potato. She sunbathed on the balcony with her friends – girls like Irene, Margot and May, the solo school of later years – and threw cherry stones at the men on their way to the Gents'. The roguish dog, lurking in the yard, was also a hazard on that journey. On one occasion a customer came marching in, pulled down his trousers and said to one of the Adas: 'Look what your bloody dog's done to me.' How many lawsuits might that lead to today – the wayward animal, the negligent owner, the lewd customer – but what actually happened was that the man sighed, resumed his trousers and ordered another drink.

And then it was time, for my grandmother, for the eyebrow pencil and the dressmaker around the corner, for the Max Factor lipstick and l'Aimant by Coty. I too was fifteen when I first served behind the bar, but her debut was completely different: it was in earnest. She was an instant hit. 'Um... well, I suppose I wasn't a bad looker. Knew how to pull a proper pint. Men always like girls behind a counter, *you* know what men are like...'

She was sensational. Later she became immensely smart and attractive, but in youth she was a beauty. Glorious. I like to picture how she must have looked, at the centre of the long counter, with her high-gloss silent film star colouring, caught in the starbursts of the pub lights. She had such a *style* – raven-black Eton crop, neck choker, sleek satin blouse beneath what looked like a man's dinner jacket, vanilla ice-cream shoulders rising out of floor-length velvet: assured beyond her years, with a cool tang of the exotic... And yet. Again, the photographs of my grandmother aged fifteen are so familiar to me that I hadn't looked at them properly for years. Now, remembering her anew, I saw something beyond and beneath her astonishing image. Thoughts of my grandmother never moved me – she was such a tough one, always – but suddenly I *was* moved, by a glimpse of uncertainty in her eyes, a yearning that she covered thereafter beneath her gallant, restless swagger. This was part of my grandmother's legend, the girl with the Louise Brooks allure who went behind the bar and never really left it; yet I felt – still feel, can't forget the bend in my heart – as though I had perceived the small shift that she had made, so early and so willingly, to be the person she became.

Then the war: and the great fiery consummation of the affair between my grandmother and the old pub. She lost her mother and her husband – not to the bombs, as happened to Margot, but to cancer and the army – and yet, how she loved that decade between the Battle of Britain and the death of her father! The town was somewhat in the firing line. A couple of factories were targeted. But the air-raid shelter was right beneath her feet – the pub's huge cellars – and into the bunker of safety came the pub customers and the neighbours, sinner and churchgoer together, sitting with their backs to the acrid barrels, in front of them a bottle of whisky and a box of dominoes. To feel the spell of the pub exerting itself in the dark, as the unearthly wail danced above, was an intimate, dreadful excitement. It was ordinariness, the accoutrements of the known world, but enclosed, deepened, reduced to a this-is-what-we're-fighting-for essence. Back in the bars after the all-clear, the ephemerality of pleasure had become more than abstraction. Every minute at the pub mattered, hedged about as it was with metaphorical barbed wire, beyond which lay the unknown.

More prosaically, the pub was a focus for slightly hysterical activity. The saloon bar was a meeting-place for the Home

Guard, who planned their manoeuvres at the round tables: 'Oh, they were lovely. They were the posh old boys. Old Aubrey, he wore a black patch...' Old Aubrey, old Fitzroy – there was always this element, just as there would later be in my grandmother's own pub, of men with big houses and drinks cabinets and club memberships, who nonetheless went for their pint, who craved that stopping-place of sanity in their day. They wouldn't have gone to any old pub – it had to be a good house – but still they wanted to go to the pub. One of them, a married man emboldened by the opportunities that war created, began an affair with a younger woman while the pair were on fire-watching duty. She fell pregnant, which was a catastrophe, war notwithstanding. Fortunately an escape route presented itself: the girl was a twin. While she holed up and waited for the man to extricate himself from his marriage, her sister assumed her identity and took over the fire-watching. A story that one would be ashamed to invent but that nonetheless happened, and that even ended happily ever after, except for the wife.

Although, she may have been enjoying her own bit of wartime mischief. Many women were. Irene, before she married the spiv publican Stan, was up to all sorts (in my father's phrase, 'a bit scarlet') and had an actual colonel in tow. Married, of course. Meanwhile the bachelor Stan was paying flagrant attentions to my grandmother. None of this war behaviour was ever mentioned in later years, when the two women lived together, although it always somehow formed a subterranean stream beneath the conversation. My grandmother had absolutely no interest in Stan; Irene probably bore more of a grudge over that benign indifference than if there had been an actual affair, but I am not sure, anyway, that my grandmother went in for affairs. Not until Victor, who was anyway more like an ally than a grand passion. I would never have wanted to ask her, it wasn't my business, and I liked her mystery too much. Certainly her natural stance was to be the recipient of favours, to be besieged: her counter was the equivalent of the high tower in a medieval tale of courtly love. After her marriage that was the way she liked it – protected and free – with the war holding her in a kind of pub limbo.

But who knows? She never *needed* men – too sure of their attention for that – yet beyond a doubt she revelled in the masculine variety that stormed like a force of nature into the pub, broad-shouldered its way deliciously to the bar and paid its revved-up homage: there were the Poles, and then there were the GIs. 'Oh, the Yanks. Oh yes – they were out of this world.' Like many people who grew up in the heyday of Hollywood, my grandmother was fascinated all her life by America. The films that she saw at the Odeon – the screwball comedies, the early musicals – had created for ever an image of the country as a miracle of space, height, cleanliness, success, newness, Art Deco frontages, girls supple with sass, men whose ranch-reared pectorals could be divined beneath their Brooks Brothers' suits. Part of Victor's appeal was that he had been to New York. And now here were actual Americans, from the land of tobacco-chewing cowboys and Clark Gable, who came to the pub bearing an apparent infinity of gifts, occasionally fighting each other in the public bar, dancing to the gramophone in the saloon bar, singing along with Bing Crosby and the Andrews Sisters (*'you've got to accen-tuate the positive...'*), flourishing their calcium-rich dentistry and rapacious chivalry. Even the timid Miss Roach, in Patrick Hamilton's *Slaves of Solitude*, has 'her' American during the war, with whom she goes to the pub and discovers the delicious joys of gin and French. Unreliable though he may be, he is a gateway that leads to something bigger than the boarding house. My grandmother was infinitely worldly by comparison, yet the sensation of seeing and hearing the GIs in her father's pub was always one of her strongest memories, the gorgeously alien within the dear and familiar, a symbol of the confidence and extravagance that came with this time in her life, the movement towards what she believed to be her prime.

There had been unexpected plenitude. Not just because of the Americans, but because the pub was a social treasure, a great trading power (no whale meat or stocking seams drawn on with charcoal for my grandmother), above all a friend. As soon as the war was over, the privations began. Beer shortages led to fisticuffs over the slops; cigarette shortages meant that the prized packets were kept beneath the counter, only available to the favoured. The fires in the long bars struggled hard against the dire winters of the late 1940s. But still, it was the pub. For those who had made it home, it was the not-quite-home of which many of them had dreamed – a pint! at a counter! served by a proper landlady! And my grandmother, moving ever closer to that status as her father retreated quietly to his sitting room, was the everyday dream made flesh.

Not long after that it was closing time.

'Once our beer was frothy, but
Now it's frothy coffee…'

From *Fings Ain't Wot They Used T'Be*
by Lionel Bart

'My friends, we will not go again or ape an ancient rage,
Or stretch the folly of our youth to be the shame of age,
But walk with clearer eyes and ears this path that wandereth,
And see undrugged in evening light the decent inn of death;
For there is good news yet to hear and fine things to be seen,
Before we go to Paradise by way of Kensal Green.'

From 'A Song of Temperance Reform'
by G. K. Chesterton

III

The old pub is now a featureless box. It is flattened and neutralised, one of those buildings that moved with the times, only to be left behind by them. Nevertheless, it is, as they used to say, lucky to be in the band at all. About half of Britain's pubs have closed in the past century, and a quarter since the early 1980s. According to a 2016 estimate there are some 52,000 in existence, although this figure will already by too high: between twenty and thirty pubs close every week.

I think now of the rural Home Counties area in which I grew up, a collection of small villages that fairly abounded with pubs twenty-five years ago. Now, within a radius of just a couple of miles, there are four that have been converted into a house or houses, one that is now an Indian restaurant, one that took on a stupid name (the Cranky Weasel), another that became an American diner (an incarnation that did not last) and two that have been demolished. These changes seemed to happen by stealth. Every so often, as I was driving back for a visit, I would perceive that oh, that pub where I once stood on the first floor balcony with a Campari and orange (I was always trying new drinks in my teens) and watched the lumbering cricketers on the green… while I was away, its identity had been obliterated. The shape was the same, the balcony where I had stood was still there; but now the fittings were painted in that subdued pistachio which denotes upward mobility, every brick stood out in that modern-old way as if the interstices had been dental-flossed, and there was a too-large, blank-looking gap between the upstairs windows, visible perhaps only to those who knew that it had once framed the golden words 'The Bell'… The pub was still there, and the pub was no more.

Those that remain, meanwhile, play every trick in the book to keep going. Quiz nights, karaoke nights, happy hours, suntrap gardens, outdoor heaters, the Ashes on TV, the 6 Nations on TV, the Euros on TV, OAP lunches for a fiver, Mother's Day, Father's Day, Christmas Day, Summer Pimm's, Winter Warmers: anything that is over and above what a pub used to be.

There is no mystery as to why this has happened, why the pure-breed pub is dying. It couldn't be simpler to understand. Things don't stay the same. A process of evolution made the pub, and that process has not stopped. People have changed, the nation has changed, laws have changed. The advent of the breathalyser in 1967, followed by a succession of increasingly tough campaigns against drink-driving; the smoking ban in 2007; the availability of alcohol in every outlet, from corner shops to garages; the cheapness of supermarket alcohol, which in the 1970s began to see off the shops that stood within the bigger pubs, and which now undercuts the pubs themselves; the sexual revolution that has rendered quaint, at best, the notion of the male drinking arena; the primacy of children; the attendant notion that most outings should centre upon the family, rather than its adult members; the demographic shifts that have created a plurality within the national culture; the upward mobility that has led people away from familiar social spheres; the marketing of leisure, which has led people on a continual quest for novelty; the all-conquering phenomenon of the coffee chain; the fascination with food; etc.

Thus listed, these read like good things. They *are* good things, on the whole. Progressive, civilising improvements. Pubs still exist, after all, but they have evolved to survive in a different world. An improved world. And anyway, who would prefer to drink in a place of fug and beer mats, dining off peanuts, tracing dot-to-dot cigarette burns in the red velveteen, seeing their reflection swoon in a green-spotted mirror, when they could be in a low-lit interior with bleached beams, surrounded by happy groups eating at scrubbed wooden tables, with a wine list of well-sourced complexity and an olives menu?

Oh, I don't know. I would.

My grandmother always thought that food made all the difference to a pub. When food became the point, the pub became something that was not quite a pub. This is not infallible doctrine: there are gastropubs steeped in atmosphere, places that she herself would have loved. Those pub precursors, the tavern and the coffee house, supplied meals. So too, indeed, did some pubs in the mid-twentieth century. Patrick Hamilton, as reliable as it gets on this particular subject, wrote of 'businessmen's lunches' served at the Friar (the best hostelry in Reading) and blotting-paper sandwiches eaten at the bar in London pubs. George Orwell's imaginary dream pub, the Moon Under Water, also offers a 'good, solid lunch' for three shillings and even has a snack counter (in fact this pub, which Orwell conjured in an essay of 1946, is a mixture of the dutifully traditional and the idealistically Shavian: it has Victorian décor, draught beer and homely middle-aged barmaids, but it also has children running from the garden and into the bars, accompanied by their mothers, on the grounds that families are a wholesome influence upon the drinking male).

Regarding food: it is stipulated in both Orwell and Hamilton that lunches are taken 'upstairs', away from the main body of the pub. The Moon Under Water's snack counter notwithstanding, food is still an adjunct; my grandmother's stance against the *centrality* of food was not therefore contrary. She took it from her father, but again he would never have adopted it against his own interests. If his customers had really wanted food, he would have supplied it. As my grandmother did, from the mid-1908s. It was the beginning of the end, but she was too pragmatic not to know that it would, otherwise, have been the end. 'Times have changed,' she said, in that fatalistic tone of hers, which increasingly contained an underlying fractiousness. 'Pub's not a bloody cayff... thing is, Dad didn't open up in the morning for a couple of old buggers sitting with a couple of bloody halves for two hours... how am I supposed to make anything on that? And I've got the lights on, the radiators on…' Victor would smoke philosophically, waiting for the storm to pass, while Irene (loving it) would make remarks of this considered kind: 'I heard old Rex and Sheila had started going to the White Horse lunchtimes, shame after all these years coming here, wouldn't think they would, would you.'

It was quite true that the pub struggled for morning trade. Oh, those effortful hours of discreet swallows and clinks; of glasses replaced upon the counter or the table in the exact position that they had occupied before, this painstaking accuracy using up another moment or two of life; of sighs, made as it were publicly, with an air of wryly defeated irony, in the hope that they would lead to conversation ('Ah well'; 'What's up then, eh?'; 'Oh just the usual, getting old, can't do much about that, can I?'; 'Stop bloody moaning then'– another minute used). These were hours spent waiting for closing time, even for the handful of customers who had been waiting all morning for opening. This, of course, was un-pub-like. Pubs are where time acquires an exquisite value. But the mornings now refused to coalesce in that essential swooning way. The butcher, the ferocious old farmer, had staggered off to drink on more celestial planes, taking with them something of the old pub quality and regretted with a lyricism that was not, on the face of it, appropriate – and yet here I am, more than thirty years on, doing the same thing. The *soigné* urban customers – the type that had arrived with a fat crunch of tyre upon gravel, importing a sense of largesse and the scent of L'Air du Temps – they had indeed, as Irene said, begun to seek food with their lunchtime drink. The ecstatic throb of spirits hitting an empty gut belonged to a headier past. 'Can't do it now,' they would say. '*Anno domini!*' For all their defiance, these people, pub people, were moving into a dimmer light, closer to the wings. If my mother and I encountered them in another setting – pushing a trolley round the supermarket, queuing in the chemist – they looked like figures from another world, their crumbling spines held up by bandbox tailoring, still expectant of courtesy and a speck of fun. 'How's Vi?' they would always say, a flash of guilt in their eyes. 'We'll be in to see her soon.' But most lunchtimes they were settling themselves into a table at the White Horse, or the Hope and Anchor, fumbling helplessly with sachets of tartare sauce and eating scampi in a basket. 'A bloody basket!' my grandmother would say. Food in a basket was not new, but until then it had been something that she could ignore. Now the brewery, polite and just short of insistent, was suggesting that she herself might consider lunchtime catering.

She knew that it was not simply a question of customers falling off their stools like parrots from perches; nor indeed of her own age. It was change. 'It's a different world,' she would say. She could still put it in its place, but despite herself she was in its clutches, just as she had been thirty years earlier, when that different world chucked her out of the old pub. In her magnificence she had maintained her own pub as an immutable entity, an unshakeable bulwark against Suez, the Summer of Love, the Winter of Discontent, the lot. And it had been easy, really, because she held the cards: people wanted their pub. This was still true, but it was no longer true in quite the same way.

I have two images of her pub, not entirely distinct, yet differing in some elusive quality of tone, of resonance. There is the warm-lit tawny one of childhood, with its voluptuous overspill of physical memory. Then there is this slightly later one, more clear-lit and precise, without that romantic sense of infinite depth and mystery, deriving from the time when my grandmother gave in and began to 'do food'. She was quite right – it did change the pub, but change was happening anyway. The food was merely a symbol of that. It must have been happening throughout my childhood, although I would not have noticed. It had started before I was born, indeed had been going on throughout the entirety of my grandmother's reign at the pub. As early as 1961, it was estimated that a pub closed almost every day. So the decline has quickened, but its inception is not recent. During the war, people had been uncomplicatedly grateful to pubs (just as they were to greyhound racing, which reached a peak of 50 million attendances in 1945 and has been dying ever since). Afterwards other things came along. The war and its mindset were over, so too any concept of gratitude to its parochial pleasures: it was time for pubs to take their place in a hierarchy that included package holidays, Berni Inns and *The Forsyte Saga*.

The process whereby pubs ceased to be the cornerstone of people's lives was slow, however. They were still loved. They still are loved. But gradually they ceased to be intrinsic to society; only to certain members of society, for example the trio on the settle in my grandmother's public bar, who now comprised the greater part of her morning clientele and whose appearance, for which she herself should have been grateful, induced a kind of irritable pity. 'Oh Christ, now for some fun,' she would mutter as she stood at the window in habitual pose, coffee cup and ashtray balanced on the top of her armchair, and observed the appallingly punctual arrival of the sad-eyed little woman and the charmless man ('Mork and Mindy', as she called them). The ex-POW – playing it cool – was always about half an hour later ('You made it then, we thought you'd found yourself a bird,' the charmless man would chuckle grimly, as the poor old boy forced his stilt-like legs across the threshold). 'I'll go out there then, shall I?' This was Irene, emerging from the shadows, her voice as dry as desiccated coconut past its sell-by date. 'Oh good old girl,' my grandmother would vaguely reply. She remained at the window, her cheek inclined against her new chihuahua (Tom and Ted having sighed their delicate last). Except at weekends, she rarely changed out of her housecoat until evening opening.

Without the ballast of unquestioned love, the absolute knowledge that it was wanted, the pub faltered. It was like a girl who had had the choice of any man and who now – with the swollen bloom fading from her – had to coax admiration from lesser suitors. Not at night: those evenings still bloomed as of old. But in the mornings there was no sense of possibility – as there had been, in the past: even when the bars remained empty and the door latches untouched, there had been the belief, always, that the trio on the settle would be swept up into something larger than themselves, that the limits of their personalities would be transcended, that this brief span of time would dimple and soften and acquire a small kindly magic to warm the rest of the day… without that belief, the sense that it held within itself something ineffable and desired, what was the pub? It was a couple of rooms where misfits gathered because a glass of beer pushed away thoughts of death. Drink could alleviate that particular reality too, of course. Nevertheless, it hovered.

Decline did not begin in the 1980s, yet there was something about that time that was inimical to pubs. It wasn't just the economic shifts, the increased business rates and land values. It was the aspirational quality that was unleashed by money-centricity, all that *Sloane Ranger Handbook* and property porn and Filofax-flaunting, which in different form is still with us. However derided and despised that period may now be, some of the change that it effected went too deep for eradication. For pubs, certainly. Put very simply, the pubs that moved with the times, that acquired wine lists and logos and a matte veneer, became a part of that brighter new world. The pubs that were left behind, that retained their connection to the bench and the sawdust, that for all their roughness remained innocent – they were implicitly the habitat of the unevolved, the victims, those who had failed to aspire.

One can overdo the retrospectivity. People did not, in 1980, suddenly remove the safety pins from their eyebrows and start dressing like extras in a Robert Palmer video. Change moves by degrees, from the subliminal to the overt; one sees it suddenly, and therefore it seems that the change itself has been sudden. For instance I remember that there was a moment, in my grandmother's pub, when it was as though all the women who had once drunk spirits were now holding glasses of white wine. I have absolutely no idea how long it took for this change to manifest itself. All I can say is that the manifestation happened in the 1980s. It was not so much a fashion as an expression of certain societal shifts. Wine signified something different from those shallow tots of gin and whisky: it was more modern, more cosmopolitan, ostensibly more healthful (the 1980s saw the start of the fitness obsession, which again did not help the pub).

Also, it was feminised. In those days men would never have ordered wine unless with food, and not always then. Women were becoming more visible within the drinking arena, not as gin-sipping adjuncts to their suave males, but as presences in their own right. The sharp division between public and saloon bar – which was as much about gender as income – became fuzzier. More women worked, more mothers worked; the great first wave of feminism was rippling through real lives. Therefore women, like men, sought their alcoholic reward and relaxation. They also, increasingly, wanted to 'eat out', not just for their lunch break but in the evening, because as workers they were disinclined to prepare dinner (as they would still have been expected to do) when they returned home. And then, as working mothers, they sought places where they could eat *en famille*. Again, the change was not sudden: women had always worked. Look at my grandmother and her friends. Look at the work done during both world wars. The percentage of women in employment did rise in the 1980s, but not noticeably until the end of the decade. Nevertheless, the perception, the imagery – the *Working Girl* power shoulders – were potent.

And it was this – the power of 'image' – that was perhaps the greatest change of all, leading as it did to self-awareness as a normal condition. Today this has reached its endgame with the smartphone. But the psychological change, the *desire* to inhabit images – to behave as if one were starring in a film about oneself, or moving around within an advert for oneself – surely began in the 1980s: when a lifestyle rather than a life became the aim, and the individual became supreme as never before.

My grandmother saw all this, and understood it perfectly without articulating it. 'Potty sod, putting himself about,' was as far as she went, when for example a man whose dream was to be identified as a yuppie entered the saloon, asked for a menu, and left with a brutal flash of Porsche key-fob on being told that food was not to be had. She blamed it all upon television. She believed that it threw back at us a vision of human nature that tampered irreparably with the reality. She herself loved watching television, but she was old enough to see life through a screen for what it was: not life. She could not have foreseen Instagram and vlogging and the rest, and would have viewed them as the products of insanity, but they are only an extension of the same premise.

In the pub, of course, simply being was enough. The pub made that special without changing it. The black lacquered wine bar, however, created an apparent infinity of shallow reflections. It was by nature self-aware, as if at any moment Adrian Lyne might drop in for a location shot. I remember a town pub that I visited at weekends from the age of about fourteen (naturally, boys were the lure; it was local to a minor public school). My friends and I spent about a third of the evening in the Ladies', rolling flavoured gloss on to our lips, brushing our hair over our faces then swooping it back again, but we loved the lively, tatty jostle of the place. I, the unbearable expert, pronounced it a very good pub. Then, one day, the King's Arms became *KINGS*: the inn sign was replaced by meretricious lettering, the pub seating by tall tables surrounded by high stools, the usual drinks by a 'menu' of indeterminate wines, the jukebox by 'Introducing the Hardline According to Terence Trent D'Arby' on repeat. This was a harbinger of what pubs would be up against, as the drinking establishment – always evolving – moved on to encompass the world of aspiration, and hapless provincial bars were rendered fit to be seen on the Fulham Road.

Country pubs like my grandmother's did, however, have an imagistic power that required no physical change, rather an exaggerated preservation of their rural *chiaroscuro*. Just as the advertising industry came up with the concept of the 'ploughman's lunch' in the 1950s in order to sell bread, cheese and pickle in a whole new way, so the country pub with its 'roaring fire' and 'gnarled beams' became ever more of an English fantasy. Symbolically, it was already a winner; nevertheless, some change *was* required. This dream pub, like those of George Orwell and the temperance set, had to serve a pie with its pint. Otherwise there was something insufficiently cosy about it – it was too manly, too reminiscent of the days of splintery benches and spit in the sawdust – too real. The notion of a pub as a place where people simply congregated, a social hub that did not need to be named as such because nobody would have doubted it, or even thought about it, all this was evaporating along with the smell of Player's Navy Cut: it was over, or as near as dammit.

Again, the change was not sudden. Pubs had been remodelled as Berni Inns since the mid-1950s, and those steak-and-chips-plus-Chianti meals were a near institution by the late 1960s. Similarly with Aberdeen Angus 'restaurants'. These chains surely influenced the way in which pubs evolved, prefiguring Harvesters – which started in the early 1980s – and their kind. But food in pubs was one thing; good food was another. This was the age of *nouvelle cuisine*, of Raymond Blanc as a semi-celebrity. The first intimations could be felt of what would become another obsession (was this, in fact, when things became obsessions?), but the gastronomic revolution had not yet gained momentum. Fifteen years later, the village pubs where I grew up would be offering ingredients such as roasted peppers (almost all of the seeds removed), balsamic vinegar, mascarpone, the usual suspects gathered together in herb-flecked groupings. At the time I am describing, the food on offer was rather more basic.

In preparation for the great Lunch Launch, my grandmother, mother and I visited another pub in the area – the White Horse, or possibly the Hope and Anchor – to see what they were up to. We had intended to be incognito, like spies for Egon Ronay, but my grandmother could not really do that. Barely had we got through the door before she was enveloped by wheedling, traitorous customers and a wary, perspiring publican. She batted away the questions as to whether she was retiring, or considering her own forays into food. She sat in her leopard-print coat, smiling with slightly alarming regality, opening her heavy gold compact to retouch her lips, as sweetly incompetent young waitresses hovered with typewritten menus and took down orders all wrong. The tables, near-weightless dark wood, bore a bowl full of semi-liquid butter pats and no cutlery. Up came the nervous landlord: 'Got your irons, Vi?' He meant knives and forks.

The food was unspeakable: my lasagne was swimming in water from defrosting. 'Makes you feel a bit Billy, doesn't it,' said my grandmother, peering into its swampy depths (she meant Billy and Dick: sick). It later transpired that everything had been stashed in the freezer straight from the cash-and-carry store, a place infamous for its cheap spirits, which certain low publicans would decant into bottles of Teacher's and Gordon's.

The conversation on the drive home – more of a soliloquy, in fact – was characterised by its repetitions ('Could you believe how/when/why...?') and its rages ('Did you see Laura's?/I wouldn't have given mine to the dog/Did you see old Rex and Sheila, looked a bit bloody sheepish didn't they...?'). It proved one thing: that the visit to this other pub had not been wasted. My grandmother's spirit had been wholly roused. If she had to give people grub, she would show them how it was done. She was a hostess, after all, and nobody west of Whitechapel made a better salt beef sandwich. 'And those bloody menus…!': she was referring to the typed sheets with their letters out of alignment, like clues in detective fiction. It was decided that my mother, who could do calligraphic writing, would produce elegant pages that would sit between leather folders. The ideas had begun to flow like fine wine. Irene would make pies and quiches. My grandmother would roast a piece of beef for sandwiches. Victor would shop for provisions, or perhaps my mother would do that better – you couldn't trust old Vic to know a decent tomato, they'd be like little red bullets if she knew him. Sally, from the next village, who had been married to old Mick, might be asked to make puddings. Sally might be asked to help with serving. Yes, it would all work out, in the end.

I remember very well the transformation that was wrought upon the pub. I arrived one morning, entering from the backyard as the pub doors were still tightly bolted. Through the open door I saw that the tiny kitchen was draped in food like an altar at harvest supper: lettuces, cucumbers, softly subsiding loaves, bags of chips, a ham edged with firm freckled fat, uncooked pies decorated with leaves of pastry. A new coffee machine, whose mind was always very much its own, stood on the shelf beneath the window. Where before the air had crackled richly, dirtily, with fried butter and fiery inhalations, now it was shot through with the smell of spring onions and clean new bread. In the sitting room Victor sat silently, glancing through his *Sporting Life*, the new dog Tom II by his side; he inclined his head towards the saloon bar with a complicit, faintly weary air of 'keep me out of it'. There, too, all was unfamiliar. The four tables had been laid with cutlery (irons) and on one of them my grandmother was ironing napkins with a heavy, pounding touch. Irene was by the counter, doing something with condiments. 'What you doing over there, Rene?' 'Filling the salt – you want salt, don't you?' She threw a few grains over her left shoulder, just as my grandmother always did. The woman named Sally, a comely divorcée in her fifties, bustled in prettily from the car park with a tray: on it were two large foil-covered dishes. 'Floating islands, Vi, and apple pie.' 'Oh darling.' Goodness, it was different.

By this time I was preparing for my A levels (I was fifteen, but my adorable school took little account of things like age; I had been two years younger than everybody else when I arrived, and simply continued to be so). Having failed at ballet and musical theatre, I was being encouraged, in a consoling spirit of 'never mind, you can always be clever', to try for Oxford. I was at the pub quite a lot in the summer holidays. It was around this time that I made my debut behind the bar. The legality of this was never questioned. I did it for money, but more importantly because I wanted to inhabit my grandmother's legend; I could scarcely wait to preside and glow as she had done.

I had not reckoned, until then, with the gulf between image and reality. What she presented, that imperishable extroversion, was something that I had absorbed without understanding. I had no idea what it felt like to be her, and no idea how to be as she was. Behind the bar I did not transmute into a smooth, gloriously capable, womanly avatar; I was me, full of the outsider's unease that was in fact my prize, my future, but that served me very ill in the face of professionally lecherous men, narrow-eyed women whispering discontentedly into their husband's jackets, spluttering beer pumps, barrels that needed changing at the least convenient moment (oh the dread of it, like a car hiccuping out of petrol), glasses that wobbled perilously as I reached them down from their high shelf, incomprehensible orders for things like 'a splash', sharp characters who eyeballed me as they said, 'No, I gave you a tenner, love,' when I handed them their change for £5, lairy characters who asked for a half in their pint glass in order to say 'put a bit more in than that, love', brain-freezes that prevented me multiplying £1.55 by three, and above all the sense that I was letting the side down.

But then, the morning pub was letting me down also. Serving for the occasional half-hour at night, as both my brother and I might be prevailed upon to do, in return for being young people with a pub at their disposal (a bit of a gift, frankly) – that was another thing altogether. It was *fun*. A divine light-heartedness overran the whole business, led by the farmers and their robust, 'What the bloody hell have you given me here, girl?' when I poured the wrong drink ('Go on then, hand it over, I'll try anything once'). Regulars like the man who tried not to pay 5p for lime in his lager, or the man who liked to recount his traumatic experiences, filled me with the ridiculous joy of seeing their myth in action. Outsiders – those who asked querulously for straws, or more ice, or a tray – also made me hilarious, surrounded as I was by insiders, people who were clocking it all and on my side. 'You should have bashed him over the head with that tray, girl. Christ, how many bloody hands do you need for a couple of drinks.' And of course I had reached an age at which every crack of the door latch had become peculiarly exciting, because at any moment somebody might walk in and fall madly in love with me, as my father had fallen for my mother.

But mornings were not fun. They were not pub-like. They were not lost in themselves. The sign outside the pub, reading BAR FOOD, did indeed cause an instant increase in the number of customers: the success was remarkable, almost absurd in its predictability. 'Well, they said it would happen, didn't they,' said my grandmother, shaking her head in unhappy satisfaction, as if over a grimly accurate Tarot reading. In fact it was entirely her own doing, just as it had been when she first arrived at the pub and created a clientele out of *almost nothing*. The food that she offered was simple yet sumptuous; quite soon the pub was listed in guides; the four tables in the saloon might be used by three different sets of customers in a morning session, and the public bar also began to demand its share of sandwiches. Although Sally was waitress-in-chief – wafting Floris scent as she passed lightly through the bars – I too dashed back and forth, watched carefully by the little woman on the settle, who would say 'Speedy Gonzalez' or some such thing as I passed by. She did this every time, and I found that I lacked the pub kindness to acknowledge her. I also found that I disliked playing servant to those whom I did not like, which was most of the new customers. I lacked the insouciance that could make the words 'sir' and 'ma'am' into semi-ironic courtly flourishes. In fact, although I did not think of it in these terms, our old friend class had entered the scene; as a member of the middle classes, I resented having to dance attendance upon members of the mimsy class.

Nor, despite the immediacy of her triumph, was my grandmother finding much joy in it. Certainly she was not making much profit. She was unable to resist overloading each sandwich with enough innards and decoration to constitute another meal; then, when customers queried the price (which they often did), she would go berserk. Her rages were instant, as they had always been, but now they also had staying power. 'Little tight-wad bastards,' she would say, cutting with quick, vicious thrusts through a couple of tomatoes. 'They've got best bloody beef, enough to feed a regiment, they're getting best butter, that's half a Cos on the side, and they don't want to pay eighty pence for it?!... What is that, Rene, in real money...?' 'Sixteen bob, Vi.' 'Sixteen bob, well, Christ. I know what they want, though. They want something cheap and nasty, out of a freezer, full of bloody water. Let 'em sod orf, then.'

And so it went on. It was summer, the broad burning stripe of the sun lay across the kitchen, and it was mayhem. Did health inspectors ever visit, I wonder? They surely must have done, but how the place ever passed I have no idea. My grandmother despised hygiene, and her longevity suggests that she had a point. Nevertheless, officialdom would have been perplexed, sorely so, by the flypapers that still fluttered within the dank larder, long orange strips pasted with winged raisins; by the ancient oven that blasted like a ship's funnel; by the Breville sandwich toaster edged with black crusts, removed periodically with a jabbing knife; by the cardboard boxes in the yard, steeped in oil, dumping grounds for leftovers; by the cloths soaking in opaque greenish water; by the bowl on the floor that contained Tom's chicken (also best quality), to which he pattered while on the alert for other nutritional possibilities. There was no dishwasher, no protective clothing. My grandmother wore a hairnet, but that was to keep her rollers in place. Her huge diamond rings, butter-smeared, left an imprint on the bread when she pressed down to cut it. Smoking was done outside the back door, but not if it was raining.

How did she manage it? I ask myself again. Again, she had help: Irene, Sally, sometimes Marian, my mother – who did indeed buy the provisions – and me, I suppose. But a person in their sixties was older then than today, and the work was relentless. The women shoved each other into all available crevices as they sought a few square inches in which to cut and prepare. The steaming air was streaked with heat haze, like a mackerel sky. Irascibility was the emotional starting point, revving up to panic, thence to despair; yet at the same time a strenuous good humour prevailed, so unnatural as to be more alarming than ill temper. It came, I realised, from Sally. Because of her sunlit smiles and constant 'jokes', my grandmother and Irene were obliged to block the culverts of their self-expression: sarcasm, speculation, thinking the worst. Only when she was out of the room could they relax and whisper comfortably together. If she was there, the conversation tended to revert to the same theme. Every smashed plate, every sliced finger oozing deep scarlet on to white bread ('No, I can't serve that, can I'), was met with a girlish cry of, 'Oh, Vi, are there any nice rich men out there to take us away from all this?!'

There probably were, as it happens. The new customers were mostly business people. But Lord were they dull. The smokeless air of the saloon was as still and flat as an official photograph compared with the colour, carelessness and ceaseless reactive energy in the kitchen. The atmosphere around the tables was calm, filled with the sounds of discreet munching and office jocularity. Ponderous considerations of the menu could go on for minutes. Sometimes one had an odd sense of antagonism, as if the new customers knew that they were not really wanted and sought to impose themselves in a muted, middle-management-style revenge; as when they queried prices, or on occasion the food itself. 'Ha, my goodness, I'm not sure I ordered quite that much fat on my ham!' The implied grievance was never pursued, merely established. If Tom the chihuahua scuttled out into the saloon, as he often did near closing time, occasionally aiming a flurry of barks at a random luncher, he was acknowledged with a tight, embarrassed bonhomie. 'Wouldn't get much of a sandwich out of that,' was a murmur that I once heard, from a man in a group of powerfully suited chartered surveyors: they were the new regulars. At the bar they cocked their heads like budgerigars and treated me to their best lines ('Well then, what do you recommend for some starving males? – don't answer that…!'). When accompanied by a female colleague, however, the script was rather different ('Hang on, love, that's got way too much head on it, hasn't it...'; 'I'll have the same again, love, in a clean glass this time...').

'Showing orf, I suppose, in front of that little broad,' my grandmother said. I had left Sally to take the interminable order. The kitchen conversations, when they were allowed free rein, were the only thing that made the lunch customers tolerable to me. As soon as I heard the familiar rhythms of my grandmother duetting with Irene – 'Well, they're having a carry-on, aren't they,' or, 'Did you see the tip? I should have told him to shove it up his you know what' – I would return to the bar with a sense of being restored to myself, as if a slug of champagne was dancing cheerily down my veins. When I went back I saw that the woman in the surveyors' party was looking up at Sally, pulling a face so bizarre that I couldn't imagine what had provoked it. Her lips were turned down, her eyes mournful as a clown. In the voice of a five-year-old she said: 'No quiche today?' Then, turning to the men: 'But oo *pwomised* Jilly quiche!'

This was too much even for Sally. I followed her back to the kitchen, ostensibly to get the black pepper, and heard her imitating the woman: '... so if there was weally weally no quiche, she would have to *make do* with a beef sandwich.' At that moment a slice carved from the joint fell to the kitchen floor, and was briskly raked by Tom's teeth before Sally could retrieve it and put it on the counter. 'I should make it with that bit, Vi.'

*

214

It was the lure of sandwiches that had brought the public bar back to life, yet as the summer wore on it rediscovered a more pub-like quality, or the insubstantial echoes of it. The trio on the settle watched it all, their faces almost featureless in the light that burst through the window behind them, throwing their hunched little bodies into blackness.

As my grandmother had done before me, I acquired a few admirers, although I felt them to be deeply inferior to those at the old pub. But there was one, a history student, from a well-to-do family – which earned me a certain respect in the kitchen conversations – who one morning behaved in a way that became part of the pub legend. He had told me, during our first chat, that he had in his possession a genuine shepherd's cloak and crook. I had no idea what 'genuine' meant in this context, nor can I recall how this subject arose. As the pub had taught me, however, I feigned flattering interest. A couple of days later he turned up wearing the cloak, which trailed imperially along the ground, and carrying the crook, which was higher than the pub ceiling and had to be propped at an angle. A scion of one of the farming families was seated by the fireplace. 'What you got there, boy?' If the young man had thought to impress with the cloak and crook, it quickly became clear that he had failed. Instead of leaving, or removing his disguise, he stood sulkily at the counter and began ordering barley wine. I had never heard anybody do this before – the dust on those bottom-shelf bottles had remained undisturbed, as far as I knew, since the three-day week – and I was aware of

the drink's reputation. A flurry of giggly alarm spread around
the bar as he ordered a third, then a fourth; through the
shadows I could see the little woman on the settle nudging
her neighbours with agitated elbows; by some osmotic
connection the news of this unprecedented event reached
the saloon, and when the young man placed a hand firmly
just an inch from the edge of the bar, collapsing into his
cloak as he requested a fifth, so Sally popped her pretty head
through the hatch and hissed: 'Vi says no more barley wine!'

The farmer took charge, sending Sally to order a taxi and
coaxing the young man out of the pub. From the window I
watched him stalk off towards the orchard, trip on the cloak
and disappear down the hill. By the time he re-entered the
car park, the taxi had arrived. There was a brief tug-of-war
with the crook, but eventually I saw the farmer insert it into
the young man's car, with its end sticking out of the window.
Both car and crook must have been reclaimed at some point.
As I recall I stayed away from the pub for a few days, trying to
live it all down, which was quite impossible with the farmers.
'Where's that boyfriend of yours? I've got a few old yowes he
could help me with...'

But this was a sideshow. The main players in the public
bar – the last such set to generate proper interest, in the pub
sense – were a group who gradually took possession of the
mornings, ordering their sandwiches with much pomp and
circumstance. At the centre was a fat, bearded, unhealthy,
extremely rich old man, a Home Counties King Lear with
a coterie of hangers-on. I never worked out who they all
were, but the kitchen conversations identified a niece plus

boyfriend, a housekeeper and a number of vague associates ('I reckon he runs that garage for him, doesn't he'). At the edge of the group was a civic dignitary, whose wife was the Mrs Big Tits to whom my grandmother would merrily wave from the window. This couple were tacitly accepted as almost the social equal of the old man, and they conversed across the rest like potentates. Everybody else was in the old man's financial thrall ('Course, she's got nothing, the niece, but I reckon she's the only family'). He bossed and dominated while they cravenly endured. 'Now then, my pretties,' he would say, 'we shall all be having another drink, shan't we, my pretty children.' He knew, of course, that thoughts of loans and handouts and wills were jangling wildly behind their fixed smiles; even I, without benefit of kitchen wisdom, could see the game that he was playing, his amusement at their eager, unhappy faces, the gratification that he gained from sitting on his stool (my grandmother's stool) and holding court. With luscious sadism he explained why death duties should be much higher, because inherited wealth was all wrong. He thrust £20 notes at his housekeeper and ordered her to buy everybody more drinks. He told jokes, often quite off-colour. When he did this, another member of the party – balding, fortyish, standing slightly apart, employed in some unknown capacity – would look at me with a sorrowing, searching gaze that I found far creepier than the jokes. He was one of those men who would wait as long as it took for a woman to meet his eye, if necessary until nightfall. 'Sorry about the jokes, my lovely, not quite what a girl like you is used to, eh.' His voice, perforce, was low. As always at these uncomfortable times, I tried to conjure my grandmother: her cool and breezy smile, her ability to dismiss without offence but with unanswerable finality. 'Oh, well...' I turned away and lit a Dunhill: a mistake. 'Oh dear, oh dear, oh dear – you don't want to be doing that, do you, does she, King Lear? Does she, with those healthy young lungs?' The old man usually ignored me rather heftily, as somebody who could not be persuaded to be in his debt in any way. 'We don't want her doing it! Do we! Might get some of that ash in our glasses, mightn't she, pretties?'

Smoking had indeed become rather rare during morning opening. Hardly anybody smoked in the saloon, and the trio on the settle had been cowed into near abstinence by the new group in the public bar, who waved their hands about like conductors of Brahms's *Hungarian Dances* if a customer lit up near their sandwiches. Backstage was another story, of course. My grandmother's bronchitis grew worse every year, but she regarded a pub without smoke as decadent.

As a diversionary tactic, however, smoking was not enough to deflect the balding man. One day he came into the pub alone. He drank a couple of pints at the counter, bowling the occasional ball towards the trio on the settle but returning, between deliveries, to face the bar and stare in his sadly smiling way. It was a near-empty morning, probably a Monday. There was nothing to constitute a diversion. As I pulled a third pint, praying that it would turn out in a way that left him nothing to remark upon, he said quietly: 'I'd like you, my lovely, to think of me as your uncle.' A pause. 'I don't have to be your favourite uncle. But I'd like to be your uncle. If you understand me.'

Oh, it was nothing, although it is the sort of thing that today one could make a furore about, and I said nothing to my grandmother about it. I felt a sense of responsibility to our shared faith in the pub, as a place where standards were implicitly understood. I also felt that running off with tales was not what one did. She would have been enraged, and I disliked the idea of her having to be. With regard to issues like my inadequate pint-pulling, she was sternly inclined to take the customer's side ('Well, they're entitled to a decent pint, I suppose'). And the folly of men was something that she knew all about; had the inappropriate behaviour happened elsewhere, as of course it did – to me, to other girls – she would have dismissed it with a knowing shrug ('Soppy sods, take no notice'). But this was an act committed not just against me, which she would have considered bad enough. It was against my status as her granddaughter, thus against herself. It was *lèse-majesté*, the kind of transgression that made her obdurate and serious. It was as if all those years of creation – of drink not drunkenness, of fun not frenzy, of hand-polished glasses, customers as friends, publicans as local celebrities, warmth and standards and no jukeboxes; all the years in which my grandmother had been treated like a queen, the counter that she stood behind circling her like a magic ring – it had all been undermined, the respect that was due to the pub, by a creepy old bastard who had no understanding of what the pub signified.

It signified less, by then. What is almost impossible to assess is how much the pub had changed, and how much my own perceptions. My real life had always been outside and beyond, but it now assumed proportions so great as to overwhelm the pub. I still liked going in there – I was, after all, a favoured regular – but its grip upon my imagination was loosening.

I had feared that my grandmother would be thrown off balance by the behaviour of the balding man; in fact it was I who found it disorientating. Not upsetting (hardly worth that). But it slithered into my head and shifted a veil through which I had observed the pub realities. Similarly, I remember an evening in which the main customers were the townspeople, six of them sitting together in the saloon. The neatly belted flared suits of the 1970s, in which they had looked so sprightly, were replaced by weightier items: double-breasted jackets and silky patterned dresses with a bow at the side of the hip. Drink was doing its work, blurring their faces. 'Oh, fuck, don't I look rough,' I heard one of the women whisper to herself, as I entered the ladies to find her painting the puffy canvas; it was a glimpse of the horror of ageing, when its measure was nothing more than one's changing reflection in the same mirror. Her eyes slid across me like lizards. I had never liked serving these people, and was gladder than ever not to be doing it.

Back at the saloon counter where I was sitting with a friend, I turned to blow smoke into the air and saw, actually saw, the moment of the car keys being thrown into the ashtray. A myth in action; I nearly said as much. Then I saw the identical expression on each man and woman's face, a perfect blend of excitement and boredom, and imagined the comments the following night, whispered into a chosen ear. 'She's a bit of a girl, blimey, isn't she.' 'He had a bit of trouble, I'm afraid, in the downstairs department.' The pub had always shown adulthood to me as many-textured, worth the wait. These people made it into – what? A series of kicks against decline and routine. I had known as much, really, but now I *felt* it.

So what, exactly, had been hallowed about it all? It had been life, no more, no less. That was the pub. It had never claimed to be anything else.

And life was different now: as was I, but it wasn't just me. The accretions of atmosphere were being slowly dispersed. There were still times when they merged and danced in the old way – parties, evenings that took flight because enough of the right people were present, evenings that became exhilarating and silly and lost in themselves – but all too often they refused, for the simple reason that the pub no longer meant what it once had. Its congregation was turning up, but without the faith. The world to which it belonged was changing; therefore even if the pub itself stayed the same – which this one did, sandwiches notwithstanding – it would still, inevitably, change because it was a performance, a mirage, vulnerable because dependent upon something it could not entirely control: the willingness to suspend disbelief.

Of course as a child I had seen visions of wonder in the fairy-grotto dazzle of the counter, and an infinite magic in the softened light of the bars. Had I been older I would have seen them differently; how differently, I cannot know. I know that I didn't imagine a place so full that one could scarcely move, the plenitude on offer, the laughter that cracked the air like thunder. Those were real, although I hallowed them. How much, again, I can't know. But memories are not only what one remembers, they are the way in which one remembers. When I think of the pub, as I knew it in childhood, the chambers of my memory instantly fill with gold; and that, therefore, is the truth of how it was. I was a spectator at the great production created by my grandmother, and like the people who saw Olivier's Richard III or Nijinsky's Derby, I am defined, in part, by the memory.

And after all, is it not in the nature of the pub to think of it elegiacally, to hallow it above its logical deserving, to shape it for the past even as one lives in its present? 'What things have we seen done at the Mermaid.' Francis Beaumont wrote that to Ben Jonson in the same spirit as my grandmother talked about the old pub, and as I now recall hers in its glory days. What is meant by it is as fluid and elusive as life itself. All I know is that I was lucky.

It was remarkable that my grandmother, who was so alert to every nuance of behaviour in her customers, did not see what was coming in her own life.

A year or so after the introduction of food, which by then was a daily norm no more vexing than a low-level hangover, she went out for an evening with Victor. This now happened far less often. Trips to London, usually to Harrods beauty salon and thence to the food hall, were managed by my mother. It still amazed my grandmother that she could not park on Bond Street or 'just pull up' outside the Sea Shell on Lisson Grove. Her loyalty to Wheeler's had been superseded by a passion for

Langan's Brasserie, which was indeed very smart and buzzy in those days, and to which we would go *en famille* for birthdays. By degrees, Victor had been absenting himself from the more feminised scene of the pub; it seemed that he had no desire to recline in the sitting-room armchair, amid thick drifts of steam and the sound of strained womanly banter; nor did he want to sit in his familiar place at the saloon counter inhaling vinaigrette. He sometimes turned up near closing time, for a Guinness and a short walk with Tom, whom he adored (as did everybody except the deadly lunchers). Then as the pub finally cleared he went off again. I hardly noticed this reduced presence because he would have seemed so out of place anyway: a eunuch in a pinafored harem.

His evening with my grandmother was not in London but at a pub a few miles away, which like so many had been run by a couple of her friends. Now their son had taken over. Full of the zest of youth, he had crossed the chasm and was offering dinner to his customers. My grandmother was extremely keen to see this in action, but the evening was not as expected: it ended in an almighty row because Victor had made a fuss, to this poor novice restaurateur, about the cooking of his steak (he was a rare-meat fetishist). He dropped my grandmother at the pub and drove straight home. My parents were there – locum publicans for the night – and to them she expressed, in her typically forceful yet meandering way, a mixture of fury, embarrassment and fundamental boredom about the whole strange incident.

Not long afterwards she went on holiday, staying with friends in the Algarve, while Irene, Victor and Sally looked after the pub. When she returned it was to the news that Victor had asked Sally to marry him.

I don't think that my grandmother minded; not at all. If anything, I think that she was relieved – she had far too high an opinion of herself to feel slighted – and in retrospect there was no surprise about what had happened. 'Oh dear,' I heard her saying to Irene. 'Poor old Sally, she was worried to death… Her poor face peering at me when she asked if I was all right about it… oh dear, oh dear. Well, he's got a few quid – decent sort of house – she's not done too badly…' It seemed to me – because I was getting a little better at these things – that Victor had been waiting nearly forty years for his revenge upon my grandmother, who had turned him down but kept him around, had wanted him but only on her own terms. He had truly appreciated her: that was beyond all doubt. I found myself thinking that he should have carried on appreciating her, for what she was, on whatever basis, instead of seeking a cosy little set-up with a banal wife fifteen years his junior and floating islands every night. Irene shared my view, rather angrily; that too I perceived. Beneath her acidity she was good to my grandmother. The bond between them was impregnable, far more than whatever had existed with Victor. Irene was family, when all was said and done, and family was at the heart of my grandmother's belief system: it was because of her father that she believed so unquestioningly in the pub. The tumour that had begun to rattle inside Irene's lung would cause her far more anguish, over the next year or so, than Victor's late-life bid for autonomy. A few months later he returned to the pub, without Sally and with an air of urbanity that he did not quite carry off; I saw my grandmother watch as he buried his papery face for a few moments in Tom's neck. She herself was blithe, fond, quite perfect. She was always able to accept when things were over; that too was part of her genius.

What I found oddest was not that Victor had turned the tables on my grandmother, because I didn't really think that he had. The true reversal was in my grandmother's role, which – as with any true publican – had always been that of observer. Now, for the first time in my life, she was the story, the person whom she would have discussed with rigorous zeal with Irene in the kitchen. 'Well, she never really wanted him, else she'd have married him, wouldn't she.' 'Well, he fancied a nice little wife, someone to look after him I suppose, didn't he.' 'Well, she was always on the lookout, eyeing up all those men who came in to lunch, wasn't she.' Did other people talk about *her* in those terms? I found the idea shocking, an affront to the natural order. Even now I find myself protecting her. I remind myself, console myself, that very few customers would have known the nature of her relationship with Victor, which over the years had become ever more detached and imprecise. I did once hear her talking to somebody about this sudden marriage of his, but she was in fact lamenting the loss of Sally – 'My lovely cook, my wonderful waitress! What am I going to do without her?'

And indeed Sally, then Irene, then all the customers who succumbed at last to a duller reality, did prove impossible to replace.

I'm not sure that my grandmother gave the pub a backward glance as she walked into the car park with Tom in her arms, leopard-print coat streaming behind her, and got into my mother's car. It was a brisk day in early spring. Also in the car were cardboard boxes packed with the paraphernalia from the sitting room: the decanters, with the silver tags slung about their necks engraved with the words 'whisky' and 'brandy'; the heavy tumblers and the bottles of good booze; the Schweppes soda siphon the Royal Albert; the records of Bessie Smith, Dinah Washington, Brenda Lee, Timi Yuro. At her feet was her blue tin box full of make-up and a bottle of champagne, which we drank that evening.

I had visited the pub a couple of times beforehand and run my hands along every possible inch of the brick and stone. I remember particularly the rough yet comforting feel of the wall along the landing, where I now had to stoop, and then the fat humid heat of the pink and marble bathroom. I remember everything, or so it seems to me, which comes to the same thing. Most of all I remember the settles, pulled away from the wall for the first time in almost forty years, leaving a complexity of spiders' webs from which hung catkins of cigarette ash. They stood in the middle of the bars with an air of obedient displacement, their ebony backs gleaming dully in the triangles of natural light, waiting to be taken to auction and thence to who knows.

Soon after my grandmother's move into my parents' house, there was a further change in the laws relating to drinking. It was no longer compulsory for pubs to close in the afternoons: for those that wished to remain open, the light-and-shade separation between matinée and evening was over. 'Christ, I'm well out of that,' she said, dealing the cards smartly for a hand of solo.

She was seventy by this time, and had spent most of what she had earned at the pub. She was intensely respectful of my father's money, without which I have no idea what would have happened to her. She never exactly displayed gratitude, however, and he certainly never sought it: he liked her too much. She paid for her keep, anyway. The large bedroom that she used is still filled with her white and gold furniture (with the leopard-print coat hanging in the wardrobe, a thin ridge of Estée Lauder foundation hardened at the neck), and the photographs from the old pub hang on the wall. She watched television in the room, with Tom by her side, absorbing anomalous hours of *Ironside*. She went shopping with my mother, spending the few thousands that had been invested for her. And as if without volition she transformed the house into an approximation of the pub: card games and drinks and worldly stories punctuated with 'oo-ers', decanters and glasses arranged once more on a cabinet in the sitting room, music swooping and swelling from the gramophone in the kitchen. She acquired a taste for sherry, and poured herself a wineglassful at around midday. Every Saturday she would try to persuade my brother, a high-level rugby player, that he should join her before going off to his match, as sherry would warm his blood for the scrum. She was still the hostess, unable to be otherwise. If a man came to read the meter, she would chuck an entire packet of biscuits impatiently onto a plate, longing to serve in that powerful old way. If friends or family visited, she let loose her personality with a kind of vast sigh. She longed, always, for an occasion to rise to, and she would fashion one out of almost nothing: a trip to the supermarket or the doctor.

I no longer lived at home, but when I visited we might go out to a pub that she had once known – 'Oh, this was old Joyce and Ray's, oh tsk, oh dear' – and that had been transmuted into something fit for the modern world. For some time, her famous presence could send publicans into a bustle of hysteria. At one establishment the food arrived on the table, and it transpired that a couple of orders for chips had been forgotten; no matter, said the proprietor, I'll get them for you; a couple of minutes later he returned, sweating as one newly released from a sauna, holding in front of his apron a deep-fat fryer from which he shook chips directly on to the plates. As time went on, however, the anxious old publicans disappeared. It became accepted that what had been a pub was now a restaurant, an informal and no worries kind of place, a not-quite-home in which Reeboks could be worn and children could squawk. Aspirational had embraced casual: what one might call a Blairite ethos.

Yet it seemed to me an unfair exchange, all that cunningly distressed wood and hey, how are you guys doing today, where there had once been a place full of intrigue and nuance and everyday mystery. I would look at my grandmother, sitting with the plate of king prawns that she now always demanded, offering up her ritual comedic rebuff to the question of whether she wanted a glass of water – 'only for washing in' – at which the nice young Badoit-flourishing waiter would look blankly perplexed, as one unsure whether or not a joke had been made, and indeed whether or not water was actually wanted by this strange, splendid, alien lady. Despite the flat vanilla sheen that the strip lighting cast over her face, I seemed to see the flickering play of memories, of Wheeler's, Isow's, Sheekey's, Jack Straw's Castle, the old pub. Sometimes she was unable to restrain herself. 'Not much, is it?' she would say, casting around her a look of cheerful benevolent contempt. The new managers did not know who she was, and this liberated her. She accepted her own obsolescence with the lively stoicism that characterised her. She accepted change with a shrug. 'Oh, it's a different world, I know that.'

She could not, however, accept the smoking ban. It didn't affect her. She had given up cigarettes a couple of years before they killed Irene, because it had seemed that she herself was the one who was suffering: every winter she was racked with an increasingly cruel bronchial cough, terrible sometimes to hear. When she left the pub, this eased immediately. My father smoked, but he alone could not create the grey mushroom cloud that had hovered over the bars at night. Nevertheless, my grandmother refused to believe in passive smoking – bronchitis was different, she said – and anyway took the view that everybody died of something, and if it wasn't fags it was probably booze or grub or bad bloody luck. She was roused to Chestertonian rage by what she saw as an attack upon freedom, and upon what was left of the pub as she had known it. '*Can't smoke in a pub?*' The images of her old home – the nicotine-dirty ceilings, the men communing intently with their pipes, the women puffing smartly on their B & H, the packets of Player's Navy Cut crumpled in the ashtrays, the blue gauze threading through the spirals of sound in her little sitting room – they were all wrapped in that lethal and lovely fog. Smoke was of the essence, it *was* the essence, and without it the pub was no longer the pub.

For all her liberalism, my grandmother was not politically correct. This mindset seemed to her quite natural, although today it would be regarded as a contradiction in terms. How could a person be without race bias – say – yet believe that a pub was a masculine environment? Which she did, unquestioningly. Pubs had a place for women, but they were places for men. Her own pub, for instance, was her personal stage. Yet she would always say that when she entered the public bar on an early Friday evening – when it had become, tacitly, the personal stage of a group of businessmen relaxing jovially over their first pint of the weekend – then the atmosphere tightened: the men became gallant, welcoming, they couldn't have been more pleased to see her, but in a barely perceptible way the fun was over. 'Oh they all loved me,' she said irritably. 'I know that, but they were much happier on their own.' This wasn't always true, of course. But she was right about this particular configuration of men. Nowadays such an idea would be regarded as an outrage; although in fact it was because these men were polite, and made her the instant focus of their gathering, that the atmospheric shift occurred – if they had chosen to ignore her, they could have carried on regardless with their happy nonsense. And indeed the arrival among them of a boring, miserable man would have destroyed their evening far more conclusively (although more effective still would have been the arrival of one of their wives; not because she was unwanted *per se*, just at that particular time).

This kind of thing, which is actually rather subtle, is now forbidden to be so. From it has arisen an image of the pub, the true pub, as a place full of blokes rendered metaphorically redundant by the brave new world, in which a landlord shakes his head over health and safety gone mad and the customers plot a sullen, xenophobic revolution of the little people that will proclaim the right to buy pork scratchings in ounces rather than grams. This pub – let us call it the Farage Arms – assuredly does exist. It is like any bad pub: colonised by its members and resistant to outsiders. It is therefore unlike the true pub, in which everybody is theoretically a member (not that this nirvana is always attained, but it is the unstated aim). Yet as modernity continues its march upon the pub, bleaching its beams and serving its food on artists' palettes, so the image of the pub as it was, in the evil old days, has become ever more identified with smoke, drink-driving, men without women: all that is past, all that is wrong, all that needs to be purged.

And again, there is some truth in this. But it is not that simple. Pubs were not simple, however much they could resolve complexity. My grandmother could not have 'defended' her belief in cigarettes, a few beers before driving, men drinking together and so on – at least not in the language of today because she would not have seen it in those terms. She could, however, do something that has become rather rare: she could separate the personal from the politicised. To her, a man who wanted a drink alone, without his family, was no more or less than that: he did not symbolise a host of other attitudes. Only if such a man were to transgress in some other way – behave, for instance, like the man who sought to become my 'uncle' – only then would she rear up and judge. Otherwise it was life, the imperfect business that the pub was there to accept. Those who sought to make life into an image of itself, and whose thought systems adhered to an ideal of perfection, were not her kind: they were not pub people.

I was with her. The influence of my past was very strong. By that time I was finding a blessed continuum with the world that she had created, drinking in places like the French House, which still contained men who would introduce themselves as a descendant of Brian Boru and take one on to the Colony (no Muriel any more, but all the same); or the Coach and Horses, where one could watch an afternoon's racing from a tattered seat with a half-pint of wine and Jeffrey Bernard in one's eyeline; or a couple of the pubs in Newmarket, where people in the know would describe the potential Guineas winner they had seen on the gallops that morning, but more importantly would talk about something other than themselves, something that lit a quick, unexpected flame. These pubs had their centrality, their *point*. They were about something more than going out in order to use up a few hours in a slightly different way. They allowed an evening to bend and breathe, as it rarely does in the known worlds of social congress, where the moment of leaving is so often the most pleasurable. Such pubs are still not quite extinct, but they are rare beasts.

Racing pubs are interesting, because horse racing (like dog racing) has much in common with the pub. Racing, too, believed unquestioningly in its power to absorb people's attention, to compel their love. It too was once so healthy as never to think about death. Now it staunches the constant slow ebb of its lifeblood. When my grandmother went to Epsom in the 1930s, the country stopped for the Derby; today almost nobody outside the sport would know the name of the most recent winners (Wings of Eagles, 2017, anybody?), and there is very little to be done about this. One cannot force a nation to bow down before an entity simply because it was once a national institution.

The solution of the racing industry has been to sell itself as something other than racing. It attracts large crowds to major meetings because these have been fundamentally reconstituted: they are open-air malls, places where people can dress up, go on the pull, buy stuff, get their nails done, watch a band, eat and, above all, drink until they fall over. Very few of these people look at a horse. Their attention is back where it wants to be: on themselves. But at least they are *there*, rather than at one of the thousands of other places that they might be. In a society in which life often resembles a multiplicity of open browser windows, there is logic to the idea of making everything like everything else.

Thus with the modern pub, which does so much that is not pub-like, and keeps alive by so doing. Yet this philosophy – that survival depends upon attracting those who do not care whether or not you survive – has generated an opposite reaction: a passionate yearning towards authenticity. The genuine racegoers – whose view of the course is obscured by people pointing their phones at a Royal Box containing Harry and Meghan – will gravitate to the purity of the Newmarket gallops at dawn. The genuine pub lovers – whose drink with a friend takes place to a jabbering soundtrack of, 'And what is the only sequel to have won the Oscar for best picture?' – will seek out the microbrewery, the craft beer tasting.

The pub is dying. Yet so many people seem to want it to stay alive. Every week more than twenty pubs close, yet one regularly hears the story of a particular pub's fight for life. The notion of the pub as the 'hub of the community' – again, an idea rich in authenticity, reminiscent indeed of the great old inns – has taken a hold upon our collective consciousness. Now that almost half of our smaller villages have lost their pub, the desire to save those that remain is becoming a minor crusade. The sense of what is being lost has been recognised, which does not mean that it will be prevented.

The paradox about authenticity is that it, too, can be commodified. Therein, perhaps, lies the pub's best chance of survival. A perfect metaphor for this was created when a generic London pub (the sort that looked as though it had, in its time, been a proper old boozer) was demolished by a property development company, even as it was in the process of acquiring listed status; local residents took the cause of their pub to Westminster Council, and the developers were ordered to rebuild the pub, brick by brick, sign by sign

(SPARKLING ALES; LUNCHEON AND TEA ROOM), remaking it in every detail as it once had been. This is a wonderful story, of course: a triumph for the London of heterogeneity against the crass grab of the corporate. Nevertheless, this pub can never truly be remade as it was; it will become a facsimile, a totem, too valuable as a signifier to retreat into the pub's sacred shuffling ordinariness. That quality, that *reality*, is what cannot be replicated.

This, after all, is a world in which a Chinese investment company bought the Plough pub near Chequers, after it was visited, in 2015, by the then prime minister David Cameron and President Xi. The intention was not to turn the pub into flats, not to destroy it, but to glorify it: to capitalise on the status of a venue where the two leaders partook of fish and chips plus pints. 'The English pub concept is growing very fast in China,' said the company's managing director. A chain of Plough-like establishments is now projected to be built in the country. The pub is regarded as a place in which to do business but, more than that, it is an attraction. It has theme-park status. Again it is a facsimile, a totem: this time of Britishness, like a double-decker or a bulldog. That is why Madonna, in her country-tweed phase, bought the Punch Bowl pub in Mayfair, and why Tony Blair took George W. Bush (a teetotaller) to the Dun Cow at Sedgefield. Would David Beckham buy a pub? He might, if public interest in his fate remains a fashionable concern.

Which it may not, of course, which anyway makes scant difference to the vulnerability of many pubs. In 2016 the government declared a desire to staunch the haemorrhage –

some 8,000 have closed in the past decade – and introduced a 'pubs code', which allowed tenants or mortgagees of tied houses (as my grandmother had been) to apply for the right to become a free house. Without the tie to the brewery, the publican could buy beer from any source and at a cheaper rate. It is not unlike the legislation that enabled people to buy the freeholds of their properties; and, unsurprisingly, the large pub companies went into action. The terms for breaking ties were made so harsh as to be almost prohibitive. A case was cited in which a putative 'free-of-tie' rent was raised to almost £50,000 a year, double what was being paid by the tied tenant.

Then came 'reforms' to business rates, leading to increases so extreme as to make national news. This tax had wrought destruction upon pubs in the 1990s, when they were far less beleaguered; yet some landlords were advised their rates would increase by as much as 150 per cent over the next five years. Again the government offered help – a discount for almost every pub in the 2017 Budget – along with a recognition that the system of business rates needed reform. Nevertheless, the position is now one in which any further pressure could close even a thriving, well-run pub.

Since the 1990s, an alternative fate has been absorption into the maw of a company like Wetherspoons, Enterprise, All Bar One, Greene King or Punch Taverns, which now own around half of our pubs. Such is the success of Wetherspoons (almost 1,000 establishments in its ownership in 2017) that, in reversal of the usual trend, it reclaims buildings such as post offices and cinemas, and turns them into pubs. The dominant chains have also bought up large quantities of failing pubs, often from regional breweries.

Some chain pubs are tenanted, some managed. Some retain their own character. But many are homogenised spaces; almost unrecognisable as pubs, in fact, with the divisions between bars ripped away – separation of that kind being not modern – and, with that literal removal, the pub's implicit guidelines also lost. In those amorphous anterooms anything seems possible: a demonstration, an orgy, a mass gin-palace-style brawl. Thus the tension between freedom and restraint, the sense of pleasure being authorised, evaporates into the smokeless, vacuous dark.

This feeling I had, that the true 'pubs code' was disappearing as if it had never been, was intensified by the Licensing Act of 2003, which dispensed almost completely with the concept of opening and closing times. I always assumed that there was a real, hidden, commercial reason behind this legislation, because it seemed utterly impossible that anybody could be so naïve as to accept the stated reason: that all-day and all-night drinking would mean no more drunkenness. Instead people would pace themselves, knowing that they would not be turned into an alcohol-filled pumpkin that would splatter on to the pavement and upset the neighbours. There would be no need to choke down one, or five, for the road, because the road would have been existentially extended. The pub would, in fact, be smoothly annexed by the cosmopolitan, café-society culture of Cool Britannia, and these words of Patrick Hamilton would become merely a part of prehistory:

A horrible excitement was upon everybody and everything... they beat their palms with their fists, and they swilled largely and cried for more. Their arguments were top-heavy with the swagger of their altruism. They appealed passionately to the laws of logic and honesty. Life, just for tonight, was miraculously clarified into simple and dramatic issues. It was the last five minutes of the evening, and they were drunk.

Well, they are still drunk. On the pavements, on the racecourses, on the beaches, at the football, the cricket, the clubs. It frankly amazes me when I read – as I did in early 2017 – that spending on alcohol had almost halved in the past fifteen years. Perhaps I go to the wrong places. Perhaps statistics are not always wholly accurate. It is true that there are factors in which one can believe: the rise within the population of religious non-drinkers; the rise of abstinence within the clean-living, clean-eating, quinoa-Instagramming young; the rise, indeed, of twenty-first-century temperance. Nevertheless... what of the tumbling, staggering bodies outside those cavernous chain pubs, the lurching figures who thump the windscreen as one inches through London traffic on a Saturday night, the glasses thrust into the camera lens at Aintree or Magaluf? *These* people, at least, are keeping up their drinking, thank you so very much: and these half-naked cavaliers are no more use to the pub than the new puritans.

Save our pub, people say. What do they mean by it? Are they dreaming of a new culture, a local clothed in the loose disguise of the pub: a place in which to meet, eat, drink beer flavoured with coffee and gin spiked with thyme, use a library, buy milk, tend allotments between lattes, play Monopoly, have a sing-song? The examples of 'community pubs', of pubs reclaimed and remade by the people who use them, are very much like that. They are smiling, friendly, family places, in spirit not unlike George Orwell's The Moon Under Water, which was perhaps conceived some seventy years ahead of its time. As with the restaurant-pubs, some of which are undeniably charming, they represent an evolution that makes societal sense. Customers want them, they take shares in them and put their best selves into them. This may not be enough, financially speaking, but they represent a continued life for the pub: one that is – 'authenticity' again – a reassuring retreat to the world of the medieval inn, with its all-purpose community aspect, just as microbrewers and micropubs (in which two or three customers congregate around a beer tap) represent a reversion to the *artisanale* world of the ale-wife and alehouse.

I am so glad that all this exists, that there is a *will* for it to exist. These places are a defence against the deluge. They are not, incidentally, my own idea of pubs. They are simply too nice. I always liked a slight tautening in the diaphragm before entering a pub, even my grandmother's. And I suspect that others share that view, almost without recognising it; that their attachment to the pub, their desires for its salvation, lie in something more numinous and mythic, in fact in a series of images: of sodden beer mats, foaming pints, velveteen seats the colour of week-old rioja, dark wood pierced with a clean sliver of sun, dust motes rising to greet the morning's first customer, a shaft of shadowy promise seen through an open door, a bar like a shining dressing-room mirror framing a landlord, a landlady. Images that in reality would no longer mean what they once did because the reality around them is no longer the same.

Does it matter? It does, yes. It is a slipping away, a seemly pressing between the pages of history of something that was once so tough, so proud, like the buoyant stride of Max Miller on to the stage of the Kilburn Empire, or the roar of the Harringay crowd when the traps opened and the dogs grabbed the turf with their greedy paws, or the beyond-delighted whoop of Brenda Lee going up the lazy river; so many things that were about a way of life, but more than that were about the engagement with that life, to which people never really gave a thought, which makes them lost to us.

I know what my grandmother would have said, that what was gone was 'gorn', but in defiance of her creed I returned to her pub, about fifteen years ago now. I had driven past it many times, of course, observed the changes that were inflicted upon it: the window shutters painted yellow, a chalkboard advertising fish and chips on Thursday nights. I still felt a memory of sweet apprehension whenever I approached it. I still had a sense of ownership, of what the hell was somebody else doing in there, treading the familiar boards.

Meanwhile my grandmother, who talked about the pub quite often, did so in the prosaic present-tense manner of the kitchen conversations. If, for instance, she saw a former customer in Morrison's, she would set off on a detective trail of 'Now who did she go orf with?/So who went orf with old Steve then?/Looks bad, doesn't she, well that's drink for you.' These people – who could never have suspected such verbal treachery, so ecstatic was she in her greetings – would still fall at her feet when they saw her: it was extraordinary. Having accepted their homage she would, however, express a certain contemptuous amusement. 'They all swore they'd never set foot in the pub again, didn't they, after I went? Bloody liars, they were straight back the next bloody week, weren't they.' However much she had valued it, she was quite unsentimental about the relationship between customer and landlady. She knew its fakery as well as its sincerity: a pub remained a pub, with or without its presiding presence; nobody knew that better than she did. When I mentioned *en passant* that I had been back there, she took it completely at face value. I had gone to the pub, what was more natural than that?

Such strange things that my memory had moved to meet. The crunching, rolling sound of the tyres on the gravel. The slope of the stones on the courtyard outside, the feel of them under my feet. The tiny little step before entering the public bar. It had to be the public bar – I had envisaged drinking in the saloon, but what I didn't know until I arrived was that the pub had taken an anxious plunge into the world of dinner, as well as lunch, and the little saloon was now filled with people eating – elbows almost jamming into their neighbours' mouths as they lifted their forks – and with the dull miasma of warm food.

The landlord looked fraught, shimmering with tension beneath his smiles, far more comfortable serving his regulars than grappling with corkscrews and Sauvignon. A woman, who had a wifely air, occasionally strode up to him and whispered something into his sideburns that he didn't want to hear. As I came out of the Ladies' – still pink-lit, still so astonishingly the same that the smell of sodden Camay bloomed briefly inside my nose – a young waitress was bustling through the wooden door that divided the pub from backstage. It was then that I saw the dining tables, three of them, neatly packed into my grandmother's sitting room. Three couples were eating their chicken in the space where the sounds of adulthood, timeless in their possession of the there-and-then, had trailed across the dusky air and through the crack in the staircase door, my slender observation post on life.

There were about ten people in the public bar, mostly drinking alone: it was a number that made it both full and not full enough. People had to be friendly, but they couldn't get friendly enough to get going. Without the settle against the wall, the seating looked to me somehow makeshift, as if in a slightly overcrowded waiting room. And the glass shelves behind the bar seemed to have lost their intensity of depth and colour – no bottle of Green Goddess; no stacked packs of Dunhill – but perhaps that was me, with my child's memory, which held a near-infinity of gleam that had never quite existed, although for me it had.

A couple of the customers knew who I was; I have no idea how. They were generic countrymen, undoubtedly related to one or other of the farming clans, and they nodded sagely at me as I waited for my drink beside the fireplace. Something did seem different there, as though a couple of items were missing. Of course the cauldron and brass poker were now at my parents' house.

I am trying now to think how I felt about it all. I felt something, strongly, but I wasn't sure what it was. I was looking around me: at the door that led to the cellar, at the golden bell above the bar, at the wall-lamp that had glowed above my grandmother's head, where in her day the flame had been a warmer red, and had always looked to me both adult and innocent. It seemed significant, this little room, what it held, the things that had changed and the things that were immutable. Significant of what? I had begun to ask myself.

The man with whom I was drinking was slightly bored, as I had expected. His expression made his thoughts perfectly clear: the place I had talked so much about, romanticised, as he didn't quite say, was no more or less than a pretty little pub with a somewhat droll clientele of yokels and *petite bourgeoisie*. Which indeed it had always been, if one looked at it that way. That, I understood, was the judgment of the world to which I now belonged, the knowing metropolitan world that regarded pubs as symbols rather than realities: as subject matter. I accepted it, with my grandmother's wry shrug, although I remember that after a couple of drinks one emotion did emerge, clear as only the right amount of alcohol can induce. What I wanted, quite passionately, was for that world of mine to fall away: for the landlady to stride out of her sitting room and put it firmly and good-humouredly into its place ('Fancies himself a bit, doesn't he, poor old Bill') and to be standing once more with her at the bar.

She was ninety-six when she died. The regime of her last years was, in most respects, contrary to received opinion about how to achieve old age: she breakfasted on toast with great quantities of butter, spent all morning cooking a splendid lunch while drinking her sherry and listening to the gramophone, sunbathed in a sarong for the rest of the day if it was hot – she had acquired a reptilian tolerance for heat in the south of France – and retreated to her armchair if it was cold.

She still came to life for social occasions, although afterwards she might spend several days in bed. A couple of years before she died we had a summer party at the house. I saw her standing outside with one of her special glasses (which could accommodate half a bottle of champagne), surrounded by a circle of wide-eyed admirers, taking a drag from a friend's cigarette. She was never diminished, not a whit. If nothing else, pride would have forbade it. If she wasn't up to amusing people, she preferred not to appear. Otherwise what had they all been for, the years of cascading her personality like confetti? She had always believed in the profundity of putting on a show, and she kept the faith with herself. As she was driven away to the hospital, a couple of weeks before she died, she waved at me through the window then made a comic *moue* and turned her thumb downwards, like a Roman.

They were all there at the funeral, the pub people, friends and relations, the ones who were still above the ground. As befitted her ferocious atheism, it was not a particularly sacred occasion. Harry Nilsson was played in the crematorium (*another bride, another groom*). I had placed a bet and, back at home, absented myself briefly to watch the race, where I was joined by a couple of similarly interested parties. The horse won, and for a quick hallucinatory moment I heard her offering me her admiration, assessing whether or not my winnings would buy a round (this had always been her measure of money: an inadequate amount always dismissed with 'that wouldn't buy you a round of drinks'). At her implicit suggestion, I had a large gin. 'Oh Christ, how bloody beautiful.'

As the afternoon sky turned aquamarine, and the funeral party thinned, I grew melancholic in the rich, luxuriant, pleasurable, spirit-drinking, tomorrow-defying way that came, by stealth, with the approach of closing time. I was not sad, except for my mother. That had not been the nature of the relationship with my grandmother. I had thought her superb, difficult, admirable, alarming, wise, self-centred. Without ever saying as much, or even realising it, I had regarded her as an ally in the business of being a woman. I was and still am somewhat in her thrall. I was not close to her, exactly, because she was a performer, an extrovert, a landlady. She was the last landlady, for those of us who knew her.

She would have been unsurprised by the coda to her funeral. By the time that darkness had claimed the sky, I was finished; I was never what she called a '*good* drinker', and a gin haze had risen in my head like the swarming of tiny bees. Yet the handful of guests who remained were, I saw, returning to dogged life. There was even, in one quarter, a hint of late-mid-life dalliance in the air.

So what might she have said, in one of her famous stage whispers, out in the kitchen with the sunken vol-au-vents and the sweet molasses sound of Dinah Washington? 'Well, course, he was after her years ago, wasn't he'; 'Um, well, she's got in the mood, hasn't she'; 'Can't blame 'em, you're only here once.'

I had gone outside with the dogs. I looked at the black velvet sky, thought of the dresses lent to Lot and Lil at the old pub, and blessed it. When I went back into the sitting room there had been a further change of atmosphere: it had shifted, brightened, was charged with a kind of stoical anticipation. The handful of remaining people were hitching themselves up, putting on lipstick, retouching, rebuttoning, readying themselves like soldiers for their last posting at my grandmother's pub.

It's only right, they said, we'd better go and have one.

Acknowledgements

I am deeply indebted to two wonderful books for some of the factual content in Part II:

Shakespeare's Local by Pete Brown (Macmillan, 2012)

London: The Biography by Peter Ackroyd (Chatto & Windus, 2000)

I am also grateful to Little, Brown for permission to quote from *Slaves of Solitude* by Patrick Hamilton (Constable and Robinson 1947).

Other brief citations are as follows:

Absolute Hell by Rodney Ackland (first performed as *The Pink Room*, 1952)

The Old Devils by Kingsley Amis (Hutchinson, 1986)

Brighton Rock by Graham Greene (Heinemann, 1938)

Twenty Thousand Streets Under the Sky, a trilogy by Patrick Hamilton (Constable, 1929–34)

Hangover Square by Patrick Hamilton (Constable, 1941)

Mr Stimpson and Mr Gorse by Patrick Hamilton (Constable, 1953)

The Strings are False, an unfinished autobiography by Louis MacNeice (Faber & Faber, 1963)

The Letters of Nancy Mitford and Evelyn Waugh, ed. Charlotte Mosley (Hodder & Stoughton, 1996)

Quartet by Jean Rhys (first published as *Postures*, Chatto & Windus, 1928)

Unbound
Liberating ideas

Unbound is the world's first crowdfunding publisher, established in 2011.

We believe that wonderful things can happen when you clear a path for people who share a passion. That's why we've built a platform that brings together readers and authors to crowdfund books they believe in – and give fresh ideas that don't fit the traditional mould the chance they deserve.

This book is in your hands because readers made it possible. Everyone who pledged their support is listed below. Join them by visiting unbound.com and supporting a book today.

Niels Aagaard Nielsen

Matt Anson

Joe Armstrong

Dena Arstall

Mary Askew

Katrina Austin

James Aylett

Paul Baggaley

Anthony Barnett

Mark Bell

Ally Bentley

Johnny Bentley

Leon Bleau

Claire Bodanis

Charles Boot

Lisa Brooke

Pete Brown

George Buchanan

Angie Burke

Joseph Burne

Carolyn Cahalane
Joseph Camberg
Lauren Carr
Ann Carrier
Clayton Chisholm
Cheah Wei Chun
Lizzie Clayson
Malcolm Coghill
Steve Comer
Robert Cox
Louise Dancause
Andrew Davison
Susan Debelle
J Mark Dodds
Maura Dooley
Owen Edmondson
Billy Ellis
Matt Emerson
Daniel Etcheverry
Rachel Fielding-Dunne
Simon Fielding-Dunne
Kim Fitzpatrick
Nick Fitzsimons
Stu Fletcher
Milo Forbes
Nico Fox
Nora Franglen
John Garrett
Tim Gee
Jeremy Graham

Vincent Guiry
Christian Hackney
Gerry Hahlo
Stephen Hampshire
Morgana Hardy
Philip Harris
Camilla Hendrick
Lucy Herz
Henry Hitchings
Tim Holt
Karen Houghton
Stan Howard
Jacob Howe
Tom Hughes
Courtney Hulbert
Robbie Isitt
Sarah Isitt
Bridey Jackson
Ali Johnson
Ruth Jones
Phil Judge
Elena Kaufman
Dermot Kavanagh
Phil Kennedy
Andrew Kenrick
Peter Kessler
Dan Kieran
Roger Kille
Chris Lee
Edie Liles

Rachel Luck

Caroline Mackinnon

Katie Maddock

Christina Marchant

Eddie Marshall

Chris Martin

Alice Mead

Paul Mercer

Luca Mighali

Peter Milburn

John Mitchinson

Katie Moffat

Alex Molden

Elinor Morgan

Michael Morgan

Zoe Morgan

Carlo Navato

David Neill

Alexander Nene

Sadie Newman

Shaz Nicol

Caroline Norton

Enda Norton

Lisa O'Connor

Tania O'Donnell

Tara O'Gorman

Victoria Page

Nick Parfitt

Richard Paterson

Sarah Patmore

Ollie Perham

Justin Pollard

Sharron Preston

Kate Pritchard

Nick Rowe

Mike Scott Thomson

Dr David A Seager

Laura Sewell

Andrew Shead

Keith Sherratt

Andy Shewan

Mischa Sokolowski

John Solomon

Ewan Tant

Joel Taylor

Maisie Taylor

Richard Thomas

Jo Thompson

George Tiffin

Adam Tinworth

Kev Toumaian

Margot Turner

John Vernon

Jose Vizcaino

Chrystine Weaver

Miranda Whiting

Sean Williams

Gretchen Woelfle

Elliott Wyndham